On the Psychotheology of Everyday Life

On the Psychotheology of Everyday Life

Reflections on Freud and Rosenzweig

Eric L. Santner

Eric L. Santner is the Harriet and Ulrich E. Meyer Professor in the Department of Germanic Studies and the Commit-
tee on Jewish Studies at the University of Chicago. He is author of *Friedrich Hölderlin: Narrative Vigilance and the Poetic
Imagination* (1986), *Stranded Objects: Mourning, Memory, and
Film in Postwar Germany* (1993), and *My Own Private Germany:
Daniel Paul Schreber's Secret History of Modernity* (1996).

The University of Chicago Press, Chicago 60637
The University of Chicago Press, Ltd., London
© 2001 by The University of Chicago
All rights reserved. Published 2001
Printed in the United States of America

10 09 08   2 3 4 5
ISBN: 0-226-73487-0 (cloth)
ISBN: 0-226-73488-9 (paper)

Library of Congress Cataloging-in-Publication Data

Santner, Eric L., 1955–
    On the psychotheology of everyday life : reflections on
Freud and Rosenzweig / Eric L. Santner.
        p.   cm.
    Includes bibliographical references and index.
    ISBN 0-226-73487-0 (alk. paper)—ISBN 0-226-73488-9
(pbk. : alk. paper)
    1. Psychoanalysis and religion.   2. Psychoanalysis and
philosophy.   3. Psychology and religion.   4. Psychology
and philosophy.   I. Title.

BF175.4.R44 S26   2001
200'.1'9—dc21

                                                    00-011852

Several people have had a substantial influence on the ideas and views presented in this book. I first encountered Rosenzweig while team-teaching a seminar with Robert Gibbs at Princeton University in 1995; I have to admit that at the time I found Rosenzweig's work to be utterly enigmatic, even overwhelmingly so. Nonetheless, Gibbs helped me to see that opening to the difficulties presented by Rosenzweig would have substantial rewards. When I moved to Chicago the following year, I sat in on a seminar on Rosenzweig taught by Paul Mendes-Flohr, who showed the way to a deeper reading of *The Star of Redemption*, Rosenzweig's principal work; Mendes-Flohr has remained a mentor in all my work on German-Jewish intellectual and cultural history. Over the next few years at Chicago my intellectual life largely revolved around conversations with two philosophers, Irad Kimhi and Jonathan Lear. This book is in large measure an attempt to work through the various questions and themes that filled those conversations. As should be clear from many of the footnotes, this book is also very much part of an ongoing relationship with the thought of Slavoj Žižek, who continues to be one of the major touchstones for my own thinking.

I also want to thank the various friends, editors, and "official" readers who, at various stages, guided me in the revisions of the book: Judith Butler, Peter Fenves, Kenneth Reinhard, Bonnie Honig, Alan Thomas, Mary Murrell, and James Goldwasser. Much of my work on this book was supported by a grant from the Guggenheim Foundation for which I am most grateful. Many thanks, too, to David Bemelmans for his meticulous copyediting. I would also finally like to thank the people whose intelligence, wit, and love framed the everyday life of this project: Deborah Nelson, Adrienne Hiegel, David Levin, Claudia Edwards, Marcia Adler, and above all and as always, Pamela Pascoe.

An early version of part of chapter 2 appeared as "Psychoanalysis and the Enigmas of Sovereignty," in *Qui Parle* 11, no. 2 (fall/winter 1999). A small part of chapter 3 appeared as "States of Emergency: Toward a Freudian Historiography of Modernity," in *Whose Freud? The Place of Psychoanalysis*, ed. Peter Brooks and Alex Woloch (New Haven: Yale University Press, 2000).

I

In recent years, as part of a more general effort to dismantle the impediments to tolerance and cross-cultural understanding in an increasingly "global" age, scholars have attempted to historicize those impediments, to provide a genealogy of their origins. The thought and hope behind these efforts is that a better grasp of the historical roots of intolerance—of patterns of ethnic, religious, and national enmity—will help people throughout the world to work through these antagonisms and establish a genuine "ecumenical" framework for living with difference. Several notable efforts in this regard have traced the origins of the most extreme forms of ethnic, national, and religious antagonism to the emergence of monotheism in the West.

In her study, *The Curse of Cain. The Violent Legacy of Monotheism*, Regina Schwartz argues, for example, that "through the dissemination of the Bible in Western culture, its narratives have become the foundation of a prevailing understanding of ethnic, religious, and national identity as defined negatively, over against others. We are 'us' because we are not 'them.' Israel is not-Egypt."[1] Schwartz is careful to note that this negative pattern of identity formation could only become a source of real violence, "could only carry force when it was adopted by groups who held the reins of power in Christendom" (x). But it is nonetheless with the system of distinctions, or rather, the system for the making of distinctions, introduced into the world through the Hebrew Bible that a new symbolic machinery for the production of extreme forms of enmity and violence entered human history. In Schwartz's view, the principle of this new symbolic machine was that of *scarcity:*

> When everything is in short supply, it must all be competed
> for—land, prosperity, favor, even identity itself. In many bibli-
> cal narratives, the one God is not imagined as infinitely giv-
> ing, but as strangely withholding. Everyone does not receive
> divine blessings. Some are cursed—with dearth and with
> death—as though there were a cosmic shortage of prosperity.
> And it is here, in this tragic principle of scarcity, that I find the
> biblical legacy to culture so troubling. (xi)

As indicated here, the exemplary instances of identity formation on the basis of a principle of scarcity involve issues of kinship, notably the giving of a blessing to only one of two siblings, a pattern clearly operative in the momentous symbolic investiture of Jacob as "Israel":

> The tragic requirement of collective identity that other
> peoples must be identified as objects to be abhorred is mani-
> fest in the violent exclusions in Israel's ancestral myths of kin-
> ship, assuming especially poignant expression in the story of
> the blessing of Jacob. Here the cost of granting a future to Ja-
> cob, that is, the cost of creating Israel . . . is literally the curse
> of his brother, Esau, the ancestor of the Edomites. . . . Struc-
> tures of inheritance, descent, and the conferral of symbolic
> property in the narrative are in the service of a system wherein
> identity is conferred at the cost of the (br)other. The Israelites
> and the Edomites cannot enjoy equally blessed futures. Like

---

1. Regina M. Schwartz, *The Curse of Cain. The Violent Legacy of Monotheism* (Chicago: University of Chicago Press, 1997), x. Subsequent references are given in the text.

the divine favor denied Cain, there is not enough blessing to
go around. (79–80)

Schwartz ends her study with an urgent appeal to reimagine the biblical narratives with a boldness exemplified by such "revisionist"
readers of the Bible as Luther, Milton, and Freud: "My re-vision
would produce an alternative Bible that subverts the dominant vision
of violence and scarcity with an ideal of plenitude and its corollary
ethical imperative of generosity. It would be a Bible embracing *multiplicity instead of monotheism*" (176; emphasis added).

In another recent critique of monotheistic religious traditions,
the well-known German Egyptologist, Jan Assmann, has also argued
that monotheism has been the single most important impediment to
cross-cultural translation, communication, and understanding, and
therefore the single most important source of negativity and intolerance in the West.[2] According to Assmann, it is only with monotheism that we encounter the phenomenon of a "counter-religion," that
is, a religious formation that posits a distinction between *true* and
false religion. Before that, the boundaries between polytheistic—or
as Assmann prefers, *cosmotheistic*—cults were in principle open, the
names of gods translatable from cult to cult because of a shared
evidentiary base in nature, in cosmic phenomena of some sort.
Translatability is, in such a universe, grounded in and guaranteed by
ultimate reference to nature. Monotheism, by contrast, because
grounded in (revealed) scripture, tends to erect a rigid boundary between true religion and everything else, now rejected as "paganism":
"Whereas polytheism, or rather 'cosmotheism,' rendered different
cultures mutually transparent and compatible, the new counter-
religion blocked intercultural translatability. *False gods cannot be
translated*" (3; emphasis added). According to Assmann, this rupture
in patterns and possibilities of cultural translation and, thus, of a
genuine cultural pluralism—a rupture that has been codified in the
West as the Mosaic distinction between Israel in truth and Egypt
in error—must be understood as a profound historical trauma, and
indeed as one that continues to haunt the West in the guise of vio-

---

2. Jan Assmann, *Moses the Egyptian. The Memory of Egypt in Western Monotheism* (Cambridge: Harvard University Press, 1997). Subsequent references are given in
the text.

lence against racial and cultural "others." Assmann's project, which he refers to as "mnemohistory" or the history of memory—here, that of the figure of Moses in the West—is an attempt to work through this trauma by retrieving the traces, from ancient Rome, to the Renaissance, to eighteenth-century freemasonry, to Freud, of a cosmotheistic legacy *within* the Mosaic tradition, a legacy rooted in the Egyptian pharaoh Akhenaten's original monotheistic innovation. Here too, then, it is a matter of retrieving from within an otherwise intolerant tradition the repressed resources of a new cultural pluralism for the global era.

I have focused on these two texts not only because they make compelling cases for the "violent legacy of monotheism," but also because both make crucial reference to Freud's work in general, and to his understanding of monotheism in particular, to bolster their cases. This book began, in some sense, with an intuition that both readers miss something fundamental in their accounts of monotheism and that this failure is directly connected to the ways in which they appropriate Freud in their efforts. The book only really started to take shape, however, once I started to read and struggle with the work of Franz Rosenzweig, above all with his principal work *The Star of Redemption* [*Der Stern der Erlösung*].[3]

Rosenzweig was, of course, one of the crucial figures in the renaissance of German-Jewish culture in the first third of the twentieth century and is perhaps best know for his work in Jewish adult education—the founding and administration of the *Jüdisches Lehrhaus* in Frankfurt—and for the translation, with Martin Buber, of the Pentateuch into German.[4] But it is the *Star* that gives us the most

---

3.   Throughout this book I cite the *Star* in English: *The Star of Redemption*, trans. William W. Hallo (Notre Dame: University of Notre Dame Press, 1985). I have made an effort to cite all non-English materials in translation. Unless noted, translations are my own.

4.   In the preface to his own new translation of the Hebrew Bible, Everett Fox expresses his debt to the approach taken (and theorized) by Buber and Rosenzweig, claiming that his own work "is in many respects an offshoot of the Buber-Rosenzweig translation" (*The Five Books of Moses* [New York: Schocken, 1995], x). Rosenzweig's productivity was cut short by the onset, in early 1922, of Lou Gehrig's disease, which eventually left him completely paralyzed, reducing his capacities to communicate to a series of eye-blinks (Edith Rosenzweig, the philosopher's wife, would recite the alpha-

powerful resources for challenging, in a philosophical idiom, the conclusions of Schwartz and Assmann as well as the vision of cultural pluralism at issue in their work, and its status as a model of ethical generosity in an age of globalization. Or more precisely, it is the *Star* read in conjunction with Freud (and Freud read in conjunction with the *Star*) that allows us to shift the ground of analysis, to rethink what it means to be genuinely open to another human being or culture and to share and take responsibility for one's implication in the dilemmas of difference. That, at least, is the wager of this book.

Indeed, I will be arguing in these pages that both Freud and Rosenzweig, albeit in distinctive idioms and with often quite divergent emphases, offer a radically different vision of the "Mosaic distinction" (and the "divine violence" it manifests, to use Walter Benjamin's phrase)[5] than the one presented by Schwartz and Assmann. In the Freudian-Rosenzweigian view I will be elaborating here, the biblical traditions inaugurate a form of life structured precisely around an openness to the alterity, the uncanny strangeness, of the Other as the very locus of a universality-in-becoming. Both Schwartz's and Assmann's understanding of cultural pluralism is, we might say, grounded in a *global* consciousness, whereas both Freud and Rosenzweig emphasize the difference, opened by the "Mosaic distinction," between the global and the universal. For global consciousness, conflicts are generated through *external* differences between cultures and societies whereas universality, as I am using the term here, signifies the possibility of a shared opening to the agitation and turbulence *immanent* to any construction of identity, the *Unheimlichkeit* or uncanniness internal to any and every space we call home. In this view, redemption (or, to use the more Freudian term: the cure) signifies not some final overcoming or full integration of this agitation but rather the work of traversing our fantasmatic organizations of it, breaking down our defenses against it. To put it another way, for global consciousness, every stranger is ultimately just like me, ulti-

---

bet and stop at the letter indicated by her husband's blinks). Rosenzweig died in 1929 at the age of forty-three.

5. Walter Benjamin coins the phrase in his essay, "Critique of Violence," in *Reflections. Essays, Aphorisms, Autobiographical Writings*, trans. Edmund Jephcott (New York: Schocken, 1986).

mately familiar; his or her strangeness is a function of a different vocabulary, a different set of names that can always be translated. For the psychoanalytic conception of universality I will be proposing here, it is just the reverse: the possibility of a "We," of communality, is granted on the basis of the fact that every familiar is ultimately strange and that, indeed, I am even in a crucial sense a stranger to myself. Freud and Rosenzweig offer us one of the most powerful conceptualizations of this strangeness as well as of forms of life open to it, indeed of strangeness itself as the locus of new possibilities of neighborliness and community.

This homegrown alterity is, as Slavoj Žižek has suggested, already palpable at the level of linguistic experience. Apropos of the elementary experience of trying to understand a word in a foreign language, Žižek writes that

> we really understand it only when we perceive how our effort to determine exhaustively its meaning fails not because of the lack of our understanding but because the meaning of this word is incomplete already "in itself" (in the Other language). Every language, by definition, contains an aspect of openness to enigma, to what eludes its grasp, to the dimension where "words fail." This minimal openness of the meaning of its words and propositions is what makes a language "alive." We effectively "understand" a foreign culture when we are able to identify with its points of failure: when we are able to discern not its hidden positive meaning, but rather its blind spot, the deadlock the proliferation of meaning endeavors to cover up.

The more general lesson of this linguistic example, Žižek continues, is that in our efforts to understand another culture

> we should not focus on its specificity (on the peculiarity of "their customs," etc.); we should rather endeavor to encircle that which eludes their grasp, the point at which the Other is in itself dislocated, not bound by its "specific context." . . . I understand the Other when I become aware of how the very problem that was bothering me (the nature of the Other's se-

cret) is already bothering the Other itself. The dimension of
the Universal thus emerges when the two lacks—mine and
that of the Other—overlap.[6]

Bringing his argument to a point, Žižek finally recalls Hegel's famous phrase: "The enigmas of the ancient Egyptians were also enigmas for the Egyptians themselves. . . . "[7] Or to anticipate a turn in
my own argument, even the ancient Egyptians suffered a form of
"Egyptomania." The crucial point in all of this is that it is precisely
when we, in the singularity of our own out-of-jointness, open to this
"hindered" dimension—the internal alienness—of the Other that we
pass from one logic of being-together to another, that we shift from
the register of the global to that of the universal which remains as such
a universal-in-becoming. The further argument of this book is that
this shift of logics marks the point at which we truly enter *the midst
of life*, that is, when we truly inhabit the proximity to our neighbor,
assume responsibility for the claims his or her singular and uncanny
presence makes on us not only in extreme circumstances but *every
day*. The cultural pluralism implied in the work of both Schwartz
and Assmann—a vision of tolerance and multiculturalism that has
become dominant both inside and outside the academy—is, I will
be arguing, actually a form of defense against this presence.

No doubt all of these issues became urgent in a new way in the
wake of World War I, at a moment, that is, when "global consciousness" collapsed into a paroxysm of national hatreds and mass death.
Rosenzweig wrote a good deal of the *Star* while stationed in an anti-
aircraft unit on the Macedonian front; a number of key Freudian
concepts—above all, the repetition compulsion and the death drive—
emerged into theoretical view only in the course of the war. The
rise of Nazism and Nazi anti-Semitism also, of course, formed the
backdrop for the writing of Freud's last completed book, *Moses and
Monotheism*, a work that figures prominently in this discussion. For
both thinkers, then, the ethical and political problem of "the Other,"

---

6. Slavoj Žižek, *The Abyss of Freedom / Ages of the World* (Ann Arbor: University of Michigan Press, 1997), 50.

7. Cited in Žižek, *Abyss*, 50.

the one who is strange to me, had immediate historical and existential urgency.[8]

II

Another motivation for the writing of this book was my sense that Freud's mostly negative assessments of religion are in some way undermined or at least challenged by what I can't help but characterize as the "spiritual" dimension of the new science he founded. My appreciation for this dynamic, that is, for the ways in which Freudian thought resonates with forms of thinking, feeling, and imagining that he sought to "disenchant," increased substantially under the impact of Rosenzweig's work.

Psychoanalysis differs from other approaches to human being by attending to the constitutive "too muchness" that characterizes the psyche; the human mind is, we might say, defined by the fact that it includes more reality than it can contain, is the bearer of an excess, a too much of pressure that is not merely physiological. The various ways in which this "too much," this surplus life of the human subject, seeks release or discharge in the "psychopathology of everyday life" continues to form the central focus of Freudian theory and practice. Now the very religious tradition in which Freud was raised, his protestations of lifelong secularism notwithstanding, is itself in some sense structured around an internal excess or tension—call it the tension of election—and elaborates its particular form of ethical orientation in relation to it. For Judaism (as well as for Christianity), that is, human life always includes more reality than it can contain and this "too much" bears witness to a spiritual and moral calling, a pressure toward self-transformation, toward "goodness." In *Moses and Monotheism*, Freud put forth a rich and highly speculative account of the genesis of this "too much" which, as he saw it, shaped Jewish life according to the pattern of an obsessive-compulsive neurosis. This study grew, in some measure, out of a deep dissatisfaction

---

8. As awkward as it can no doubt appear, I will, in the course of this book, write "Other" with a capital "O" to underscore and to keep in view the *problem* of alterity, the *question* of what makes another human being or culture strange.

with this view—a dissatisfaction that went beyond the usual and often facile criticisms of Freud's cultural speculations—but it was one I could only fully articulate once I began to read Rosenzweig.

By, as it were, reading Freud under the influence of Rosenzweig—and vice versa—I have tried to develop further what I take to be the ethical conception of ordinary or "everyday" life implied in both bodies of work, a conception of what it means to be answerable to another human being, to be responsive to the Other's claims on me. To put it in the most basic terms, I want to propose that the ethics at the core of both psychoanalysis and the Judeo-Christian tradition (as interpreted by Rosenzweig) is an ethics pertaining to my *answerability to my neighbor-with-an-unconscious.* What makes the Other *other* is not his or her spatial exteriority with respect to my being but the fact that he or she is *strange,* is a *stranger,* and not only to me but also to him- or herself, is the bearer of an internal alterity, an enigmatic density of desire calling for response beyond any rule-governed reciprocity; against this background, the very opposition between "neighbor" and "stranger" begins to lose its force. I furthermore want to propose that it is precisely this sort of answerability that is at the heart of our very aliveness to the world. The various ways in which that aliveness comes to be assumed—or refused—frame what I want to call the *psychotheology of everyday life.* For in the view I am distilling from the work of Freud and Rosenzweig, God is above all the name for the pressure to be alive to the world, to open to the too much of pressure generated in large measure by the uncanny presence of my neighbor. The peculiar paradox in all of this is that in our everyday life we are for the most part *not* open to this presence, to our being in the "midst of life." Everyday life includes possibilities of withdrawing from, defending against, its own aliveness to the world, possibilities of, as it were, not really being there, of dying to the Other's presence. The energies that constitute our aliveness to the world are, in other words, subject to multiple modifications and transformations.

Against this background it makes good sense that both Freud and Rosenzweig, not unlike a number of other modern thinkers, orient their thought around the various ways in which we remove ourselves from this midst, the ways in which we *defend* against this very sort of aliveness.⁹ And as I have already indicated, for both thinkers it is *fantasy*, that peculiar admixture of imagination and energy, intensity and rigidity, that plays the central role in these defenses; for both, then, the relevant "therapy" will involve a labor of traversing, of working through, the fantasies that in one way or another close us off from the midst of life, keep us, as it were, from living everyday life as on a holy-day. (The counterintuitive paradox I will be concerned with in these reflections is, then, that what distinguishes the holiday from the everyday is a certain *suspension* of fantasy—call it the exodus or Sabbath from our "Egyptomania"—rather than some sort of escape from the ordinary into a wish-fulfilling realm of fantasy.)

Freud and Rosenzweig are, then, emphatically post-Nietzchean thinkers in the sense that for them human life includes a surplus that is no longer referred to a life beyond this one, an Elsewhere where the "true" life would be possible. The "death of God" is in large measure just that: the death of such an Elsewhere, such a "beyond" of life that would in some sense be "higher," more real, than this one. What both Freud and Rosenzweig help us to grasp is that with the "death of God" the entire problematic of transcendence actually exerts its force in a far more powerful way in the very fabric of everyday life. What is *more* than life turns out to be, from the post-Nietzschean perspective, immanent to and constitutive of life itself. Freud and Rosenzweig are, as I hope to show, among our most important thinkers of this immanent transcendence.

9. One thinks, for example, of the logic of authenticity in Heidegger's work. In *Being and Time*, authenticity is conceived as a way of allowing ourselves to be *recalled* into the finitude of our existence manifest—and yet for the most part forgotten or refused—in our everyday dealings in the world. What is missing from this conception and emphasized in the Freudian-Rosenzweigian perspective is the centrality, within everyday life, of the uncanny presence of the Other-with-an-unconscious. The latter perspective is, in other words, an emphatically ethical one.

CHAPTER ONE

In the Midst of Life

I

In his short story, "The End of the World," Robert Walser tells of a child's search for the outer limits of the space of human habitation we call the world: "A child who had neither father and mother nor brother and sister, was member of no family and utterly homeless, hit on the idea of running off, all the way to the end of the world."[1] Possessing no belongings, the child simply picks up and begins its single-minded pursuit:

> On and on it ran, past many sights [*Erscheinungen*], but took no notice of the sights it passed. On and on it ran, past many people, but took no notice of anyone. On and on it ran, until nightfall, but the child took no notice of the night. It gave heed neither to day nor night, neither to objects nor people, gave no heed to the sun and none to the moon and every bit as little to the

---

1. Robert Walser, *Masquerade and Other Stories*, trans. Susan Bernofsky (Baltimore: Johns Hopkins University Press, 1990), 101. Subsequent references are given in the text.

> stars. Further and further it ran, neither frightened nor hun-
> gry, always with the one thought in mind, the one notion—
> the notion, that is, of looking for the end of the world and run-
> ning till it got there. (101)

In the course of its wanderings, the child entertains various fantasies as to the nature of its goal:

> On and on the child ran, imagining the end of the world first
> as a high wall, then as a deep abyss, then as a beautiful green
> meadow, then as a lake, then as a polka-dotted cloth, then as a
> thick, wide paste, then simply as pure air, then as a clean white
> plain, then as a sea of bliss in which it could rock forever, then
> as a brownish path, then as nothing at all or as something the
> child itself, alas, couldn't quite identify. (101)

As we might expect, the project doesn't go well. But after much searching, the child comes upon a farmer who, knowing that a farmhouse nearby is called "End of the World," informs the child that its goal lies only a half-hour's walk away. Exhausted from its travels, the child finally arrives at what the farmer's wife confirms to be "the end of the world." Upon awaking from much needed sleep, the child, who we now learn is a young girl, asks if she might stay at the farm and be of service to the family. She is taken into the home of the farmer's family, at first as a maid but with the promise of a future as a genuine member of the clan: "It set heartily about its chores and went diligently to work [*Es fing an fleißig zu werken und wacker zu dienen*], and so was soon liked by everyone, and never did the child run off again, for it felt at home" (102).

Franz Kafka, who was a great admirer of Walser's work, left among his papers a short prose sketch, not longer than a paragraph, to which Max Brod gave the title "The Top" [*"Der Kreisel"*]. It tells the story of a philosopher who sought after groups of children playing with a top, imagining that were he to seize the toy in the midst of its rotation he would discover universal truths. "For he believed that the understanding of any detail, that of a spinning top, for instance, was sufficient for the understanding of all things [*genüge zur*

Erkenntnis des Allgemeinen]."[2] Unlike the child in Walser's story who seeks out the limits of the macrocosm, Kafka's philosopher is obsessed with the microcosm: "Once the smallest detail was understood, then everything was understood, which was why he busied himself only with the spinning top" (444). The philosopher's project assumes, more visibly perhaps than was the case with the child of Walser's story, the aspect of an interminable repetition compulsion:

> And whenever preparations were being made for the spinning
> of the top, he hoped that this time it would succeed: as soon as
> the top began to spin and he was running breathlessly after it,
> the hope would turn to certainty, but when he held the silly
> piece of wood in his hand, he felt nauseated. (444)

The project's repeated failures generate a quasi-psychotic state in the philosopher whereby he begins to assimilate to the properties of the object of his fixation: "The screaming of the children, which hitherto he had not heard and which now suddenly pierced his ears, chased him away, and he tottered like a top under a clumsy whip" (444).

I cite these two disarmingly simple prose texts, both written within a few years of one another—Walser's was published in 1917, Kafka's likely dates from 1920—because they introduce us into what I take to be one of the central preoccupations of the two German-Jewish thinkers I discuss in this book, Sigmund Freud and Franz Rosenzweig. The problem is that of inhabiting the midst, the middle of life. In the case of Walser's young girl we witness something on the order of a flight from the middle (in her case, of course, this middle is a radically impoverished one; nonetheless, neither of these stories are conceived as psychological narratives). The pursuit of the end of the world, of the outer limit of the space of meaningful life, is, as Walser indicates in the list of the various ways the girl imagines the nature of this limit, fundamentally fantasmatic. The structure of this fantasy corresponds here to the ways in which Kant defined metaphysics in his critical writings. It is the search for some sort of "be-

---

2.   Franz Kafka, "The Top," trans. Tania and James Stern, in *Franz Kafka. The Complete Stories*, ed. Nahum Glatzer (New York: Schocken, 1971), 444. Subsequent references are given in the text.

yond" of the space of meaning that would nonetheless be a possible object of (meaningful) experience. The girl appears, in other words, to subscribe to the metaphysical fantasy that the world is itself a container-like *something*, a possible object of experience with properties like those of other objects in the world. A more mundane and common analogy would be the fantasy of witnessing one's own conception (or funeral), that is, of occupying the place of an impossible gaze at the outer limits of one's being-in-the-world.

In Kafka's text the metaphysical dimension of the activity in question is explicitly marked as such: a philosopher is in search of the Universal, the General, the Concept. The philosopher's mistake is homologous to that of the girl in Walser's text. The philosopher appears to be in the thrall of a fantasy that the universal principle he seeks can be attained from a position outside the everyday activities that make up a human life, in this case, the children's play with the top. Like the girl, the philosopher seeks to occupy a place outside of life, beyond the limits of meaningful activity; from there he seeks to grasp what underlies that life in the form of a universal principle of motion informing it and, indeed, the All.[3]

II

In a now famous letter written to his cousin Rudolf Ehrenberg in November 1917, Franz Rosenzweig explicitly distinguishes his understanding of being-in-the-midst-of-life from what he takes to be the concept of the human subject, its life, and world found in philosophy. "The concept of order of this world," he writes, "is thus not

---

3. As Stanley Cavell has summarized Wittgenstein's critique of philosophy, "For Wittgenstein, philosophy comes to grief not in denying what we all know to be true, but in its efforts to escape those human forms of life which alone provide the coherence of our expression." "The Availability of Wittgenstein's Later Philosophy," in *Must We Mean What We Say?* (Cambridge: Cambridge University Press, 1995), 61. It would, of course, be worthwhile to expand the present study to include Wittgenstein who, at some level, also understood his project as that of working through the metaphysical fantasies that distort our sense of what it means to be in the midst of life. Instead I will simply allude, now and again, to some of the parallels between the Freudian–Rosenzweigian perspective and the Wittgensteinian view of the everyday or ordinary as it has been elaborated in Cavell's work.

the universal, neither the *arche* nor the *telos*, neither the natural nor the historical unity, but rather the singular, the event, *not beginning or end, but center of the world*."[4] And in language that seems to span the idioms of Walser's and Kafka's narratives, Rosenzweig further distinguishes his conception of this "revealed" world from the "conceived" or "conceptualized" world of the philosophers:

> From the beginning as well as from the end the world is "infinite," from the beginning infinite in space, toward the end infinite in time. Only from the center does there arise a bounded home in the unbounded world, a patch of ground between four tent pegs, that can be posted further and further out. ("Germ Cell," 57)

Rosenzweig's decision, in 1920, to turn down the possibility of an academic career as a professional historian—he had written a brilliant dissertation on Hegel's political philosophy under the supervision of Friedrich Meinecke—represents the existential dimension of these philosophical concerns with the difficulties and complexities of opening to the middle of life—of, as it were, avoiding the temptations to which Walser's little girl and Kafka's philosopher succumb. Rosenzweig clearly began to experience the entire academic enterprise as a kind of defense against the exigencies of being in the midst of life, the forms of answerability he was coming to associate with it. In the letter he wrote to Meinecke who had offered him a lectureship in Berlin, Rosenzweig explains the "dark drive" that now, as it were, binds him to a patch of ground between four tent pegs (Rosenzweig had, by this time, decided to dedicate his life to the project of Jewish adult education in the context of the new *Jüdisches Lehrhaus* in Frankfurt). As Rosenzweig tells it, this drive emerged in the context of a breakdown: "In 1913 something happened to me for which *collapse* [*Zusammenbruch*] is the only fitting name. I suddenly found myself on a heap of wreckage, or rather I

---

4.   The letter has, in the scholarship on Rosenzweig, assumed the status of the *Urzelle* or "germ cell" of his *magnum opus*. See "'Germ Cell' of the *Star of Redemption*," in *Franz Rosenzweig's "The New Thinking*," ed. and trans. Alan Udoff and Barbara Galli (Syracuse: Syracuse University Press, 1999), 57.

realized that the road I was then pursuing was flanked by unrealities." Of the academic road he had been traveling, Rosenzweig writes that it "was the very road defined for me by my talent, and my talent only. I began to sense how meaningless such a subjection to the rule of one's talent was and what abject servitude of the self it involved."[5]

What made it possible for Rosenzweig to become the master of his talents rather than being mastered by them was his discovery of the persistent vitality of the Judaism he had earlier decided to leave behind as a moribund form of life, one that had been definitively superseded by Christianity. The story is well known: before converting to Christianity, as had so many of his close friends and relatives, Rosenzweig had decided to enter more deeply into his Judaism so that he could "enter Christianity as did its founders, as a Jew, not as a 'pagan.'"[6] In the course of his preparations he underwent a change of heart that very likely only became fully clear to Rosenzweig himself—only fully became "for itself"—after attending Yom Kippur services at a small, orthodox synagogue in Berlin in October of 1913. A few days after this experience he wrote to his cousin Rudolf Ehrenberg, who had already converted, the following "confession":

> I must tell you something that will grieve you and may at first appear incomprehensible to you: after prolonged, and I believe thorough, self-examination, I have reversed my decision. It no longer seems necessary to me, and therefore, being what I am, no longer possible. *I will remain a Jew.*[7]

Against this background, we can better understand the terms in which Rosenzweig, in his letter to Meinecke, relates the story of his 1913 collapse and recovery, which is the story of a breakdown that became a life-defining breakthrough. At first, Rosenzweig em-

---

5. Cited in *Franz Rosenzweig. His Life and Thought*, ed. Nahum Glatzer (Indianapolis: Hackett, 1998), 95.

6. Ibid., xvii.

7. Cited in ibid., 28 (emphasis added). This entire study is in some sense an effort to understand the notion of "remaining" as it is employed here and in related contexts.

ploys an extended metaphor, that of contracting into himself, of withdrawing, as he puts it, to "a place whither talents could not follow" and where an "ancient treasure chest" whose existence he had never forgotten but which he had never fully explored was found to contain his "most personal possessions, things inherited, not borrowed. . . . " For Rosenzweig, the upshot of this self-contraction was the impossibility of pursuing an academic career as an intellectual historian: "The one thing I wish to make clear is that scholarship [*Wissenschaft*] no longer holds the center of my attention, and that my life has fallen under the rule of a 'dark drive' which I'm aware that I merely *name* by calling it 'my Judaism.'" One of the effects of this "rule" was, as Rosenzweig put it, that he was now "more firmly rooted in the earth" than he had been when he wrote *Hegel and the State* under Meinecke's supervision. One aspect of this new rootedness (correlative to the "rule of a 'dark drive'") was an enhanced capacity to find value in the mundane details of everyday life: "The small—at times exceedingly small—thing called [by Goethe] 'demand of the day' [*Forderung des Tages*] which is made upon me in my position at Frankfurt, I mean the nerve-wracking, picayune, and at the same time very necessary struggles with people and conditions, have now become the real core of my existence—and I love this form of existence despite the inevitable annoyance that goes with it." And in language that recalls the conclusion of Walser's story, Rosenzweig writes, "Cognition [*Erkennen*] no longer appears to me as an end in itself. It has turned into service [*Dienst*], a service to human beings. . . . " Finally, Rosenzweig links this transformation to one pertaining to the very substance of his attentiveness to and curiosity about the world; his language furthermore suggests that it was made possible by, or perhaps more accurately, was coterminus with a passage through and beyond a certain *fantasmatic* structure:

> Cognition is autonomous; it refuses to have any *answers* foisted on it from the outside. Yet it suffers without protest having certain *questions* prescribed to it from the outside (and it is here that my heresy regarding the unwritten law of the university originates). Not every question seems to me worth asking. Scientific curiosity and omnivorous aesthetic appetite

mean equally little to me today, though I was once under the spell of both, particularly the latter. Now I only inquire when I find myself *inquired of.* Inquired of, that is, by *men* [*Menschen*] rather than by scholars. There is a man in each scholar, a man who inquires and stands in need of answers. I am anxious to answer the scholar *qua* man but not the representative of a certain discipline, that insatiable, ever inquisitive phantom which *like a vampire* drains him whom it possesses of his humanity. *I hate that phantom as I do all phantoms.* Its questions are meaningless to me.[8]

In these last remarks, Rosenzweig touches on a paradox that will concern us throughout this book, namely, that the release from a ban or "spell," the liberation from the driving force of a repetitive and insatiable, even vampire-like pursuit—a pursuit, we should note, framed by a specific institutional formation—is effectuated by what Rosenzweig, in language borrowed from his professor, affirmatively characterizes as a "dark drive." The drivenness of Rosenzweig's scholarly pursuits—call it his *Wissenschaftstrieb*—is counteracted by something that he still wants to call a drive. Recalling his remarks about phantoms and vampires, there is, in other words, a certain uncanny animation—what I would like to call an *undeadness*—proper to what Rosenzweig, in his own case, characterized as the life of the talents; but there is another aspect or sort of drive energy that Rosenzweig sees as precisely that which allowed him to unplug from the rule of that life.[9] The emergence of Rosenzweig's dark drive,

---

8. Cited in ibid., 96, 96–97 (emphasis added). Cavell has characterized the "poverty" to which Wittgenstein's later thought aspires in terms that strongly resonate with Rosenzweig's decision to leave behind the life of *Wissenschaft:* "First, in beginning with the words of someone else—in choosing to stop there, in hearing philosophy called upon in these unstriking words—the writer of the *Investigations* declares that philosophy does not speak first. Philosophy's virtue is responsiveness. . . . Its commitment is to hear itself called on, and when called on—but only then, and only so far as it has an interest—to speak." *This New and Yet Unapproachable America. Lectures after Emerson after Wittgenstein* (Albuquerque: Living Batch Press, 1989), 74.

9. It is no doubt important that this possibility of unplugging from the rule of the talents only truly became available to Rosenzweig on the occasion of a Yom Kippur service, that is, on a day when each individual undergoes a kind of subjective destitution, a stripping away of one's historical-cultural predicates, thereby isolating the kernel of one's answerability before God.

which he clearly experienced as a new source of vitality and humanity, as enabling his opening to the midst or middle of life, was thus correlative to a *deanimation of the undeadness* that had both driven and burdened his scholarly pursuits.[10] There is, in a word, often a thin line between the passions infusing our engagement in the world and our defenses against such engagement, between what is genuinely enlivening in the world and what is "undeadening" in it, generative of a disturbing surplus animation, not unlike the king's "second body" posited by theorists of sovereignty.[11] Rosenzweig's life and work were in large measure a meditation on that line, though I believe that this only becomes fully clear when we read Rosenzweig with Freud, when we understand the "phantoms" from which Rosenzweig was trying to unburden himself in light of a psychoanalytic theory of fantasy and defense.

III

In his short book, *Understanding the Sick and the Healthy* [*Das Büchlein vom gesunden und kranken Menschenverstand*], which he wrote at the urging of friends as a kind of nontechnical introduction to his notoriously difficult *Star of Redemption*, Rosenzweig explicitly links the

10.   Rosenzweig's letter to Meinecke can be read as a kind of critical acceptance of many of the claims made by Max Weber in his famous lecture of 1919, "Wissenschaft als Beruf" ("Scholarship as Profession"). The lecture largely addresses the impotence of scholarship with respect to fundamental decisions about value, meaning, and ethical orientation, an impotence Weber affirms as constitutive of the destiny of modernity. For Weber, this affirmation involves—and here Weber cites the same Goethean phrase that Rosenzweig did in his letter to Meinecke—a turn to the "Forderung des Tages" or "demands of the day"; this turn must for its part be sustained by a kind of drive: the turn to the "demands of the day" is, as Weber writes, "straightforward and simple if each one finds the *daimon* which holds the threads of his life and obeys it." Max Weber, *Gesammelte Aufsätze zur Wissenschaftslehre* (Tübingen: J.C.B. Mohr, 1988), 613. Weber argues that this turn involves a passage beyond what he characterizes as the Judaic posture of remaining behind, of waiting (for new prophetic leadership and guidance). For Rosenzweig, of course, it was the acceptance of his *daimon* that led back to Judaism, that made it possible and necessary for him, precisely, *to remain* a Jew, to remain one who remains.

11.   See Ernst H. Kantorowicz, *The King's Two Bodies. A Study in Medieval Political Theology* (Princeton: Princeton University Press, 1957).

latter project to a therapeutic paradigm.[12] One senses, of course, that Rosenzweig had himself suffered from the sickness diagnosed there, which he refers to as an acute *apoplexia philosophica*. And indeed, *Understanding the Sick and the Healthy* takes up the issues presented in the letter to Meinecke and formulates in general terms the cure that in Rosenzweig's specific circumstances allowed him to disengage from the specters of *Wissenschaft*, to make the shift to a very different sort of institutional and libidinal economy.

For Rosenzweig, to be subject to those specters meant to hold oneself at a distance from life and its temporal flow, to live life in the manner of the quasi-psychotic philosopher of Kafka's parable who tries to grasp the unity of life from a place outside of the temporally articulated "language games" that constitute ordinary life. As he puts it in the *The Sick and the Healthy*, the error involves the inability to let go of experiences of wonder that punctuate the current of daily life. The philosopher is unable to wait for life itself to bring the solutions to his marveling, to integrate his wonder into the very fabric of living. Instead, the philosopher becomes in some sense addicted to it as his be all and end all—as the promise of a key to the All, to Being in its totality. Apropos of the enigma of sexual difference, for example, Rosenzweig writes that its "normal solution" is found in the experience of love: "Woman is aroused by man and man submits to woman. But even as they marvel at each other the solution and dissolution of their wonder is at hand—the love which has befallen them. They are no longer a wonder to each other; they are in the very heart of wonder" (40). The philosopher, however, is unable to wait for such solutions:

> His kind of wonder does not differ from the wonder of others. However, he is unwilling to accept the process of life and the passing of the numbness wonder has brought. Such relief comes too slowly. He insists on a solution immediately—at the very instant of his being overcome—and at the very place wonder struck him. He stands quiet, motionless. He separates his experience of wonder from the continuous stream of life,

---

12.   Franz Rosenzweig, *Understanding the Sick and the Healthy. A View of World, Man, and God*, trans. Nahum Glatzer (Cambridge: Harvard University Press, 1999). Subsequent references are given in the text.

isolating it. . . . He does not permit his wonder, stored as it is, to be released into the flow of life. He steps outside the continuity of life and consequently the continuity of thought is broken. And there he begins stubbornly to reflect. (40)[13]

For Rosenzweig, this is the advent of all metaphysical thinking, thinking concerned with knowledge of the "essence" of things, with the question as to what things *actually are:*

> A thing receives a character of its own only within the flow of life. The question, "what is this actually?", detached from time, deprived of it, quickly passes through the intermediary stage of the general term and comes into the pale region of the mere "thing" [*des Dinges überhaupt*]. Thus emerges the concept of the one and only substance, the "essential" nature of things. The singleness and particularity of the subject [*Eigenheit des Gegenstandes*] detached from time is transformed into a statement of its particular essence [*Eigentlichkeit des Wesens*]. (41)

As Rosenzweig finally notes, none of this would be of any consequence were it not for the fact that metaphysical thinking is not limited to professional philosophers. "But as it happens," he writes, "any man can trip over himself and find himself following the trail of philosophy. No man is so healthy as to be immune from an attack of this disease" (42). That is, the lure of metaphysical thinking doesn't befall everyday life from the outside; everyday life is itself congenitally susceptible to this mode of thinking which is, as Rosenzweig suggests, a kind of withdrawal from, a kind of fantasmatic defense against, our being in the midst or flow of life. Rosenzweig undoubtedly felt that in modernity these defenses, this peculiar autoimmunity, had assumed the status of the norm.

At the end of the *The Sick and the Healthy*, Rosenzweig argues that the metaphysical temptation that leads one to assume a stance at the "end of the world," outside of life, is ultimately an expression of death anxiety:

---

13.   In Stanley Cavell's succinct terms, this gesture, which defines the epistemological stance of modern philosophy—Rosenzweig calls it "the old thinking"—can be understood as an attempt to convert metaphysical finitude into a determinate intellectual lack of some sort. See *Must We Mean What We Say?*, 263.

> We have wrestled with the fear to live, with the desire to step
> outside the current; now we may discover that reason's illness
> was merely an attempt to elude death. Man, chilled in the full
> current of life, sees, like that famous Indian prince, death wait-
> ing for him. So he steps outside of life. If living means dying,
> he prefers not to live. He chooses *death in life*. He escapes
> from the inevitability of death into *the paralysis of artificial
> death*. (102; emphasis added)

This "paralysis of artificial death" is another way of naming what I
have characterized as the undeadness that had, according to Rosenzweig's own testimony, constrained his capacities by burdening them
with an uncanny sort of surplus animation. We are dealing here with
a paradoxical kind of mental energy that constrains by means of excess, that leaves us stuck and paralyzed precisely by way of a certain
kind of intensification and amplification, by a "too much" of pressure that is unable to be assumed, taken up into the flow of living.
But as Rosenzweig indicated in his letter to Meinecke, the cure for
this stuckness will involve not so much an elimination of this pressure as a way of opening to it. If life includes a dimension of "too
much," then being in the midst of life will of necessity involve a
mode of tarrying with this unassumable excess rather than repeti-
tively and compulsively defending against it. To use a Freudian formulation, it will involve a certain readiness to feel anxiety.[14]

As I have been suggesting, Rosenzweig's project bears certain
startling similarities to that of Freud's, the central and most obvious
one being the thought that human beings as self-interpreting ani-
mals can become enmeshed in specific sorts of interpretations that
hinder life, cause pain, constrain life's possibilities to an intolerably
narrow sphere of movement. For both thinkers, human life produces
symptomatic torsions, fundamental fantasies that knot the fabric of
meaning within which it unfolds and for both thinkers these fantasies can be understood as fundamentally defensive structures. As Rosenzweig's discussion of "wonder" indicates, they can be understood
as hypercathected enigmas that become, as it were, *rigid with energy*

---

14.   Freud develops this notion in conjunction with reflections on trauma in
Beyond the Pleasure Principle, a work written around the same time as *The Star of Redemption*.

and keep us from opening to the temporal flow of life even though they are in some fundamental way immanent to, constitutive of, everyday life. A further parallel is that both thinkers, albeit in radically different ways, associated their distinctive therapeutic projects with their Judaic inheritance. In Freud's case, this association became more explicit toward the end of his life, above all in his last completed book, *Moses and Monotheism;* in Rosenzweig's case, as we have seen, this association constituted the inaugural moment of his mature intellectual and spiritual life.[15]

This book is an attempt to bring these two projects, which have never been seen as inhabiting the same intellectual universe, into a sustained "conversation." The result of this conversation will be, I hope, not only a new awareness of the theological dimensions of Freudian thought and an appreciation of Rosenzweig's significant and nowhere recognized contributions to the psychoanalytic theory of the drives; my ultimate hope is that when we read Freud and Rosenzweig together we will find ourselves more deeply aware of and open to what I refer to as the *psychotheology of everyday life.* As I have already indicated, this awareness is an achievement that can be understood along the lines of the psychoanalytic conception of "working through," the affect-laden process of traversing and dismantling defensive fantasies, the structured undeadness that keeps us from opening to the midst of life and the neighbor/stranger who dwells there with us. To put it in somewhat different terms, I am interested in the ways in which both Freud and Rosenzweig give us the means to think the difference between holding ourselves responsible for *knowing* other minds and accepting responsibility for *acknowledging* other minds in all their insistent and uncanny impenetrability (Rosenzweig is interested in this shift from knowing to acknowledging not only with respect to other minds but also with regard to worldly

15.   In spite of this more profound link between Rosenzweig's project and Judaism, Rosenzweig himself insisted that the *Star of Redemption* was not a "Jewish book" but rather a "system of philosophy." See his essay, "The New Thinking," in *Franz Rosenzweig's "The New Thinking,"* ed. Udoff and Galli, 69. The concepts of creation, revelation, and redemption, so crucial in the *Star,* are, as we shall see, not deployed in any dogmatic or strictly "theological" way but are used instead to capture the temporal, existential, and ethical dimensions of being in the midst of life. For Rosenzweig, the "new thinking" was thinking open to the midst of life.

being more generally—what he calls *creaturely* being—as well as to divinity; what is crucial for Rosenzweig is that both world and God have their own forms of uncanny insistence to which we can be open or against which we can erect defenses).[16]

The discussion as a whole moves between different levels and aspects of fantasy and defense: the formation that Rosenzweig dubbed the "old thinking" and that we can understand more generally as metaphysical thinking, in which the thinker is placed outside of life, at the "end of the world"; the fantasies that underlie our political and ideological captivation, that sustain our psychic entanglement with regimes of power and authority, our psychic attachments to existing social reality; and finally, the fantasies that were of primary interest to Freud in his work with individual patients, that is, the fantasies that testify to the impasses of desire as they emerge in the context of an individual's fateful passage through the straits of oedipal normativity. Though there are important differences between these kinds and levels of fantasy, there is, I think, far more to be gained by exploiting what they share than in treating them in isolation. For what is at stake in all of this are the various ways in which human beings, in their everyday life, turn away from the challenges and claims of what is in their very midst.

---

16.   Cavell has written extensively on the distinction between knowing and acknowledging. In his new introduction to Rosenzweig's *The Sick and the Healthy*, Hilary Putnam takes up Cavell's understanding of this distinction as key to Rosenzweig's project. Apropos of Cavell's reflections on the skeptic's preoccupation with the problem of the existence of the world and of other minds—a preoccupation that recalls Rosenzweig's notion of the metaphysician's mode of "wonder"—Putnam writes, "It is true that we do not 'know' that there is a world and that there are other people . . . but not because (this is the skeptic's misunderstanding) we 'don't know' these things. In ordinary circumstances, circumstances in which neither doubt nor justification is called for, our relation to the familiar things in our environment, the pen in our hand or the person in pain whom we are consoling, is not one of either 'knowing' or 'not knowing.' Rather, Cavell suggests, it is one of *acknowledging* (or, sadly, failing to acknowledge). Our task is not to acquire a 'proof' that 'there is an external world' or that our friend is in pain, but to *acknowledge* the world and our friend. I suggest that we read Rosenzweig, the religious thinker, as adding that it is our task to acknowledge God (indeed . . . he does not think one can acknowledge any one of the three—God, Man, and World—as they demand to be acknowledged unless one acknowledges the other two)." Putnam, "Introduction" to Rosenzweig, *Understanding the Sick and the Healthy*, 9–10].

CHAPTER TWO

From the Reign of the Undead
to the Blessings of More Life

I

In a brilliant and, I think, insufficiently appreciated essay on Freud, Harold Bloom situates Freud's conception of love somewhere in the interstices of Greek, Judaic, and Roman culture.[1] On the one hand, Bloom suggests that Freudian Eros is more Judaic than Greek, "since Freud interprets every investment of libido as a transaction in the transference of authority" (147) whose ultimate point of reference is the Jewish God. Indeed, Bloom goes on to claim that Freud's infamous reduction of religion to the longing for the father, for the blessings of paternal authorization, "makes sense only in a Hebraic universe of discourse, where authority always resides in figures of the individual's past and only rarely survives in the individual proper" (161). This is the thought of "a psychic cosmos, rabbinical and Freudian, in which there is sense in everything, because every-

---

1. Harold Bloom, "Freud and Beyond," in *Ruin the Sacred Truths. Poetry and Belief from the Bible to the Present* (Cambridge: Harvard University Press, 1987). Subsequent references are given in the text.

thing already is in the past, and nothing that matters can be utterly new" (152). But on the other hand, Bloom argues that Freud's very conception of authority is more Roman than Judaic:

> Yahweh is not an authority, which after all is a Roman conception and not a Jewish one. An authority founds and augments, as Freud founded and augmented, but Yahweh is a creator, a revealer, and a redeemer, whose attributes yield us the blessings of more life, rather than those that ensue from the foundation and augmentation of institutions. (160)

Bloom concludes this remarkable passage by referring to the modern thinkers whose influences come together in Freud's most audacious cultural speculation, *Moses and Monotheism*, where Freud makes ample use of this ostensibly pagan and imperial conception of sovereign power and authority to produce a psychoanalytic account of Jewish ethnogenesis, the emergence of the universe of Judaic values:[2] "Freud may be said to have assimilated Mommsen on Roman law to Helmholz on physical law, and then to have compounded both with his own vision of the Egyptian Moses as founder and augmenter of Judaism" (160–61).

These are very dense, even oracular pronouncements, and it will take me some time to unpack them. But let me state at the outset what I take to be the stakes of these remarks. First, Bloom offers the prospect of understanding the unconscious as the psychophysical inscription of the procedures—and impasses—of symbolic investiture and legitimation, procedures that are bound up with the notion of sovereignty. The unconscious, in other words, forms the locus of psychic activity whereby a human being becomes a "subject" by metabolizing its existential dependency on institutions that are in turn sustained by acts of foundation, preservation, and augmentation. And by "institution" I mean all sites that endow us with social recognition and intelligibility, that produce and regulate symbolic identities. In the view condensed in Bloom's cryptic remarks, the

---

2. The truth of this history, as Freud admits, has a different status than that of conventional historiographical constructions. For a detailed discussion of this matter, see my "Freud's *Moses* and the Ethics of Nomotropic Desire," *October* 88 (spring 1999): 3–41.

transference, this central feature of psychic life and therapeutic efficacy, ultimately revolves around the enigmatic processes and procedures whereby a human life becomes authorized, placed in a relation to the resources of value and legitimacy that constitute the very "stuff" of sovereignty. The transference is where and how what Lacan referred to as the "discourse of the Master" gets under our skin.[3] But Bloom also suggests—and this is a more original claim—that Freud's misunderstanding of the nature of authority in Judaism blinds him to the thought that Judaism might in fact be a specific and radical intervention into these very processes, that Jewish monotheism in some fashion removes itself—"unplugs"—from the enigmatic seductions of sovereign power and authority; that if indeed the Jewish God is a kind of Master, he is one that, paradoxically, suspends the sovereign relation.

Our question here will be where to locate the specific intervention of psychoanalysis, whether in the form of clinical, therapeutic practice or of cultural critique: Does it belong on the side of investiture and the predicaments of legitimation, that is to say, is the ultimate goal of the analytic cure a renewed capacity to metabolize the "stuff" of sovereignty, to assume the symbolic mandates that determine our identity in the eyes of community and tradition, our part within the social body? Or does it belong, rather, on the side of a break with the culture of legitimation and its ultimately violent cycles of foundation, preservation, and augmentation (and if so, what might a life oriented by such a break look like)? The thought here is that of the difference between, on the one hand, an *identity* mediated by institutional resources of recognition and authorization—an identity that locates us and determines our part within a socially intelligible whole—and, on the other hand, the *singularity* we assume thanks to what the biblical traditions understand as the blessings of

3.   Apropos of this notion of authorization, Giorgio Agamben has noted that in Latin, "*auctor* originally designates the person who intervenes in the case of a minor (or the person who, for whatever reason, does not have the capacity to posit a legally valid act), in order to grant him the valid title that he requires." See Agamben, *Remnants of Auschwitz. The Witness and the Archive*, trans. Daniel Heller-Roazen (New York: Zone Books, 1999), 148. What Agamben leaves out of his discussion of the *auctor* are the ways in which his acts, which certify or validate, which grant life "to what could not live alone" (150), implant, as it were, a surplus life in the one thereby authorized.

divine love. The conceptual space of this inquiry can thus be thought to span the divide between the *sciences of symbolic identity* and an *ethics of singularity*.

II

Freud's crucial breakthrough, the feature that distinguishes his conception of the unconscious from all previous attempts to think this "other scene," is, as Jacques Lacan has often emphasized, that unconscious mental activity has something mechanical, something machine-like about it. This is why interpretation that remains strictly within the register of sense, of the practical unity of life as a space of reason, is helpless before the insistence of unconscious formations which are ultimately insensitive to the question: "Why are you doing that?" Psychoanalysis is in some sense born with the perplexity apropos of symptomatic behavior, with the reflexive breakdown it generates. Thus from the *Project* on, Freud emphasized the persistence, within the dynamics of symptom formation, of a nonsemantic kernel—in his commentary on his dream of Irma's injection, Freud refers to it as the "navel of the dream"—that can only be approached by a discourse and practice attuned to the quantitative "energetics," to the psychophysical dimension of symbolization "below" the level of intentionality. This is why any understanding of repression as a form of bad faith or self-deception, that is, of merely competing propositional contents, one of which we manage to hide from ourselves but that is still, in principle, responsive to the question "Why?," will always miss the distinctive feature of the Freudian discovery. In Lacanian terms, unconscious mental activity—*symptomatic agency*—is, at its core, organized around *signifiers* rather than full-fledged meanings, beliefs, purposes, or propositional attitudes.[4] There is, in the

---

4. This is the meaning of Lacan's distinction between the moralist tradition, culminating in Nietzsche's *Genealogy of Morals*, and the Freudian discovery which radically alters the meaning of the thought that "human behaviour as such is deluded." Jacques Lacan, *The Seminar of Jacques Lacan. Book II. The Ego in Freud's Theory and in the Technique of Psychoanalysis: 1954–1955*, ed. Jacques-Alain Miller, trans. Sylvana Tomaselli (New York: W.W.Norton, 1991), 10. Self-delusion in Freudian terms does not simply mean that we somehow hide from ourselves our true motivation understood as a distinct propositional attitude.

Freudian view, something about mindedness itself that is "mindless," nonteleological, that cannot be captured by our normal understanding of what meaningful, purposeful behavior is like. The persistence of a mindlessness immanent to mindedness—a persistence that typically causes the subject a certain amount of pain (or rather, pleasure-in-pain)—is what Lacan ultimately means by the term *jouissance*. A first definition of fantasy would be, then, the specific way in which a subject organizes this *jouissance*.

The misunderstanding to be avoided here, as these last remarks indicate, is to think of the mechanical, nonsensical nature of symptomatic agency on the model of some sort of physiological mechanism—say, the beating of the heart or the rhythms of breathing—which can, of course, also be considered to be "nonsensical" or mindless. Framed by such a misunderstanding, Freud's famous dictum, *Wo es war, soll Ich werden*, would then mean that the task of analysis is the molding, the domestication of the primitive, quasi-biological energies of the drives into rational capacities and behaviors, the transmutation of the natural, "pulsational" core of life into flexible emotional orientations in a shared world. Analysis would be, in a word, a form of *Bildung*, the operator of a developmental narrative of progress. Given Freud's profound involvement with the ideology of *Bildung*, it is certainly tempting to read his theoretical gestures—in a word, to historicize them—as indices of that involvement.[5] But Freud's conception of the mechanistic aspect of the mind as manifest, for example, in the primary processes and the repetition compulsion, clearly pertains to the dimension of meaning itself and not

5. It is not hard to imagine the further directions of this historicist approach to Freud qua *Bildungsideologe*. Psychoanalysis itself comes to be viewed as a German-Jew's means of "passing," of converting a primitive, "asiatic" *Ostjudentum* into a civilized, Western habitus. The symptom would be the persistence of "fixation points" or left-overs of that passage westward, a marker of what is recalcitrant to or "indigestible" by the "process of civilization." There is, no doubt, a great deal of merit to this reading; its limit, however—and this is, perhaps, the limitation of much of the work that goes under the name of "cultural studies" today—is that it remains at the level of the *imaginary* mapping of more complex *symbolic* processes that can only be understood by reference to a more radical conception of the "indigestible remainder." What is indigestible is, ultimately, neither pure nature nor merely the remnants of another (more "primitive") culture; in a word, *it can neither be naturalized nor historicized*. I ultimately argue that this "remnant" is the place of an opening to *what is neither nature nor culture*.

to some more primitive, biological substratum of meaning. The subject of psychoanalysis—what I have referred to as "symptomatic
agency"—begins not with biological life but rather where biological
life is amplified and perturbed by the symbolic dimension of relationality at the very heart of which lie problems of authority and
authorization. To borrow a term from Giorgio Agamben, we might
say that the life that is of concern to psychoanalysis is *biopolitical* life,
life that has been *thrown by the enigma of its legitimacy*, the question
of its place and authorization within a meaningful order.[6]

Our question, then, is how we are to understand this peculiar
form of animation, the quasi-mechanical insistence, that distinguishes biopolitical life, that comes to a human life by way of its
habitation of the dimension where, as Agamben puts it, "sovereignty
borders . . . on the sphere of life and becomes indistinguishable from
it."[7] But we will also be concerned with the question whether it
might be possible to view the "blessings of more life," which Bloom
associates with the biblical conceptions of creation, revelation, and
redemption, as an opening beyond—as an *exodus* from—a life captured by the question of its legitimacy.[8] As I have already indicated,
one way in which this capture takes place is through a sort of metaphysical seduction. To be thrown by the enigma of legitimacy is to
be seduced by the prospect of an *exception* to the space of social reality and meaning, by the fantasy of an advent, boundary, or outer
limit of that space that would serve as its constituting frame and
power, its final, self-legitimating ground. The exodus I have in mind
is, thus, not one from ordinary life into a space beyond it but in a

---

6. I am following Giorgio Agamben's revision of Foucault elaborated in *Homo
Sacer: Sovereign Power and Bare Life*, trans. Daniel Heller-Roazen (Stanford: Stanford
University Press, 1998).

7. Ibid., 11. Agamben suggests that we glimpse biopolitical animation in its
pure form, at the zero degree of any political content, in the figure of the *Muselmann*
of the death camps.

8. An understanding of "exodus" more familiar to modern secular subjects corresponds with what Kant characterized as the goal of all enlightenment: the free use of
one's reason. We can call this the Socratic way, the way of philosophy. The problem, of
course, is that we are addressing a form of capture that is often resistant to the intervention of reason. We might say that psychoanalysis—and, I suggest, a certain kind of
theology—have resources in the service of "exodus" beyond the scope of reason.

sense just the opposite: a release from the fantasies that keep us in the thrall of some sort of exceptional "beyond."

III

On a first approach, we might note the ambiguity of the series of terms used in psychoanalysis to characterize biopolitical animation, the surplus vitality that in some sense *is* the unconscious. According to Freud, the crucial and most difficult task of the psychic apparatus, functioning according to the pleasure principle, is to discharge excitations emerging from the environment and from within. Both of these terms—"discharge" and "excitation"—are, however, peculiarly hybrid in nature, belonging to a semantic field of energetics as well as of intersubjective events and meanings. An excitation is a kind of pure stress, a pressure or tension in the body demanding some form of release. But in a more literal sense, an *ex-citation* denotes a summons, a calling out, and so a form of address or interpellation. The same, of course, goes for "discharge." Not only do we speak of discharging excess energy but also of discharging one's duties and responsibilities, that which one has been *charged* with doing. And to be "charged" can, of course, mean to be filled with energy as well as to be accused of a crime or "filled" with a symbolic mandate (this same ambiguity can be heard, for example, in the German word *Ladung*, which signifies not only an electrical charge but also a summons, an order to appear before a magistrate). What we need to hear in this semantic hybridity is the necessity of Freud's own hybrid discourse, which is always one of relationality as well as one of energy and its motility, discharge, and binding (we might, ultimately, think of this as the psychoanalytic version of quantum theory's treatment of light under its two seemingly opposed aspects, wave and particle).

In *Moses and Monotheism*, this semantic hybridity comes to the fore where Freud invokes the theory of trauma to make sense of the uncanny compulsiveness he discerned at the heart of what we might call Jewish spiritual functioning. In the course of his presentation, he uses an expression devised to capture the purely *quantitative* aspect of trauma, its status as a "too much" of pressure that interrupts the working of the pleasure principle, the patterns of diffusion and discharge that constitute human mindedness in its normal functioning. Every trauma must, Freud says, contain something on the order of an "excess of demand," a *Zuviel von Anspruch*.[9] An "Anspruch" can indeed signify a demand or claim as in a *demand for work* placed on a system. But the word is derived from the verb *ansprechen*, which means to *address an other*, to demand or call for the other's attention and response. We might say, then, that at least under certain circumstances a trauma is generated by a *too much of address*, by an excess immanent to an address that resists metabolization, that is symbolically "indigestible." To bring the two meanings of *Anspruch* together we can put it this way: a trauma becomes possible when a "too much of address" persists beyond what can be *translated* into a demand for work, a task to be discharged, *something we can do* (or, for that matter, refuse to do, feel guilty for not doing, and so on). More precisely, trauma ensues when such a "remainder" precipitates a breakdown of this very operation of translation, leaving the mind flooded by excitation. As Jonathan Lear has recently put it,

> [f]or Freud, the fundamental mental molecule was an idea-plus-quota of energy (which he called affect). It was the transfer of this energy along varying paths of ideas that allowed Freud to explain the formation of neurotic symptoms and dreams. In this use, psychic energy seems to be the "matter" of a form-and-matter unity. But, then, how could there be a case of pure, formless matter? How could there be *mental* energy without an idea? I think the answer is to take this as a limit case of the mental—somewhat analogous to treating zero as a number. The reason for doing this is to capture the phenomena of trauma and of momentary breakthroughs: these are vicissitudes of the mental.[10]

We might phrase it this way: Freud's crucial insight was that desires and wishes are fundamentally *interpretations* of excitation, pressure,

---

9. Freud, *Moses and Monotheism*, in *The Standard Edition of the Complete Psychological Works of Sigmund Freud*, ed. and trans. James Strachey (London: Hogarth Press, 1953–74), 23:73; German from the *Studienausgabe*, ed. Alexander Mitscherlich, Angela Richards, et al. (Frankfurt am Main: Fischer, 1982), 9:522.

10. Jonathan Lear, *Happiness, Death, and the Remainder of Life* (Cambridge: Harvard University Press, 2000), 111–12.

tension states, as having been caused by a determinate lack of some sort, by something having gone missing. A desire or wish can, in turn, occasion a number of activities, among them dreaming, symptom formation, and slips of the tongue. But by the 1920s, when Freud began taking more seriously the phenomenon of repetition compulsion, he came to believe that no interpretation ever comes off without a *remainder*, a "surplus cause" that persists beyond any determinate lack and its possible satisfaction, that is, beyond the workings of the pleasure principle.[11] Fantasy is the name for the process that "binds" this remainder, converts it into a support of social adaptation, a way of being in the world. I am suggesting that the task of truly inhabiting the "midst of life" involves the risk of an unbinding or loosening of this fantasy as well as the social bond effectuated in it.

IV

One of the thinkers who has most lucidly addressed this hybridity of Freudian terms, their dual citizenship in the "world" of energetics and the world of normativity, is Jean Laplanche. Over the last decades, Laplanche has elaborated and refined his fundamental contribution to psychoanalytic theory, the notion of the "enigmatic signifier." Laplanche has, one might say, made it his life's work to correct a certain defensive tendency within psychoanalysis itself to close in on itself by neglecting, even disavowing, the constitutive impact of the Other in the generation of symptomatic agency (this mode of defense is, in some sense, the very function of the ego). In Laplanche's terms, this is the failure to sustain the "Copernican" dimension of psychoanalytic thought, a retreat into a "Ptolemaic" or ego-centered view of the psychic apparatus. More specifically, it means the attempt to abandon the concept of seduction, the traumatic encounter with the dense, enigmatic presence of the Other's desire as constitutive of

11.   Although Freud came to this discovery by way of the traumatic neuroses, *Beyond the Pleasure Principle* represents Freud's attempt to generalize this discovery, that is, to posit such remainders as constitutive of "normal" mental functioning. Put differently, the traumatic neuroses bring to light that the mind is in some sense always operating under conditions of posttraumatic stress; the kinds of stress discovered in the traumatic neuroses are, in other words, now seen to be homologous to the stress that is constitutive of human mindedness.

the inner strangeness we call the unconscious. Because adult minis-
trations to an essentially helpless child are always permeated by this
enigmatic quality, seduction is, in a very broad sense, *constitutive* of
the adult–infant relation. The vital, alimentary exchange of nursing,
for example, is able to secrete a "surplus value" of infant sexuality
only because, as Laplanche puts it, "there is the instrumentality of
the breast, which cannot be other than an enigmatic message,
charged as it is with a pleasure both unknown to itself and impossible
to circumscribe." [12]

In an earlier presentation of this "primal scene" of the birth
of sexuality out of the *disturbed* spirit of the alimentary, Laplanche
emphasizes the interrogative core of this sexuality, the correlation
between sexuality and the entrance into a human life of the fateful
question of its place in life, which for the child means, first and foremost, its place in the desire of its primary caregiver:

> Can analytic theory afford to go on ignoring the extent to
> which women unconsciously and sexually cathect the breast,
> which appears to be a natural organ for lactation? It is incon-
> ceivable that the infant does not notice this sexual cathexis. . . .
> It is impossible to imagine that the infant does not suspect
> that this cathexis is the source of a nagging question: what
> does the breast want from me, apart from wanting to suckle
> me, and, come to that why does it want to suckle me? [13]

What Laplanche is describing here is nothing short of the birth
of the drama of legitimation as constitutive of human subjectivity.
Primal scenes are, in other words, the stuff of fantasmatic elabora-

---

12. Jean Laplanche, *Essays on Otherness*, ed. John Fletcher (London: Routledge, 1999), 128.

13. Jean Laplanche, *New Foundations for Psychoanalysis*, trans. David Macey
(Oxford: Basil Blackwell, 1989), 126. In a discussion of the primal scene of the child
witnessing parental coitus, Laplanche puts it this way: "[T]he primal scene only has its
impact because it bears a message, a giving-to-see or a giving-to-hear on the part of
the parents. There is not only the reality of the other 'in itself,' forever unattainable
(the parents and their enjoyment) together with the other 'for me,' existing only in my
imagination; there is also—primordially—the other who addresses me, the other who
'wants' something of me, if only by not concealing intercourse. What is it this father
wants of me in showing me, letting me see this primal scene, even if only by taking me
to a field to witness animal coitus?" (*Otherness*, 78).

tions not because they promise an answer to the question of biological origins—that would transform fantasy into a sort of *Naturphilosophie*—but rather because they bear fateful questions pertaining to my place and value in the desire of the Other. The fundamental situation, as Laplanche puts it, is

> an encounter between an individual whose psycho-somatic structures are situated predominantly at the level of need, and signifiers emanating from an adult. Those signifiers pertain to the satisfaction of the child's needs, but they also convey the purely interrogative potential of other messages—and those other messages are sexual. These enigmatic messages set the child the difficult, or even impossible, task of mastery and symbolization and the attempt to perform it inevitably leaves behind unconscious residues. . . . I refer to them as the source-objects of the drives.[14]

As I have already indicated, because the "vital order" of a human infant is, in its essence, defined by extended and absolute dependency on adult caregivers, exposure to enigmatic messages and the labor of their metabolization—up to the traumatic failure of this very labor—are *constitutive* of that vital order or at least, to use a different idiom, *anticipated in its creation*. Wherever we locate this "profound perturbation of the regulation of life,"[15]—a perturbation that is also a *potentiation*, that is, one without which we wouldn't have

14. Laplanche, *New Foundations*, 130. Slavoj Žižek has underlined this dimension of the message in a dream reported by Freud: "This radical intersubjectivity of fantasy is discernible even in the most elementary cases, like that (reported by Freud) of his little daughter fantasizing about eating a strawberry cake—what we have here is by no means a simple case of the direct hallucinatory satisfaction of a desire (she wanted a cake, she didn't get it, so she fantasized about it . . .). That is to say: what one should introduce here is precisely the dimension of intersubjectivity: the crucial feature is that while she was voraciously eating a strawberry cake, the little girl noticed how her parents were deeply satisfied by this spectacle, by seeing her fully enjoying eating it—so what the fantasy of eating a strawberry cake is really about is her attempt to form an identity (of the one who fully enjoys eating a cake given by the parents) that would satisfy her parents, would make her the object of their desire. . . ." Žižek, *The Plague of Fantasies* (London: Verso, 1997), 9. Žižek seems to have misremembered the dream of strawberries Freud reports in the *Traumdeutung*. The insight, however, remains valid and important.

15. Lacan, *Seminar* II, 37.

a human life—we are left with, in Laplanche's words, "internal alien-ness . . . held in place by external alien-ness; external alien-ness, in turn, held in place by the enigmatic relation of the other to his own internal alien. . . . "[16] My induction into the socio-symbolic order thus has little to do with my learning a language—that would reduce this process to a fundamentally *cognitive* achievement and relation, however stressful we might imagine it to be—but rather with and through the encounter with the enigma, my *ex-citation* by the other's internal alienness that fixes the destiny of my own desire. We are, in a crucial sense, placed in the space of relationality not by way of intentional acts but rather by a kind of *unconscious transmission* that is neither simply enlivening nor simply deadening but rather, if I might put it that way, *undeadening;* it produces in us an internal alienness that has a peculiar sort of vitality and yet *belongs to no form of life.* What I am calling "undeadness" is thus correlative to the encounter—above all in the life of the child—with the Other's desire and the seemingly endless drama of legitimation it inaugurates.[17] What

16. Laplanche, *Otherness*, 80. According to Žižek, Lacan himself wavered as to the location of this fundamental perturbation: "This problematic also enables us to throw some new light on a certain fundamental oscillation in Lacan: what comes first, the signifier or some deadlock in the Real? Sometimes, Lacan presents the traumatic colonization of the live body by the parasitic symbolic Order as the primordial fact: it is the intervention of the Symbolic that derails, throws out of joint, the natural organism in its balanced circuit, transforming natural instincts into a monstrous drive that can never be fully satisfied, since it is condemned to the eternal 'undead' returning to its path, insisting forever in an obscene immortality. At other times, in a more speculative-mythical mode, he is searching for some kind of natural excess or imbalance, a malfunctioning, monstrous derailment, and then he conceives the symbolic Order as a secondary in(ter)vention destined to 'gentrify' this monstrous excess, to resolve its deadlock." Žižek, *The Fragile Absolute or, Why Is the Christian Legacy Worth Fighting For?* (London: Verso, 2000), 91–92. My point is that once we understand that the vital order—the live body—of the human child is *essentially* open to this perturbation, we are really no longer faced with two fully distinct versions of its genesis.

17. For Laplanche, this drama gets played out above all in the domain of the sexual: "'Psychical reality' is not created by me; it is invasive. In this domain of the sexual, there is too much reality at the beginning; and it is to this 'too much reality' that the model of the 'project for a scientific psychology' can be applied: the ego processes part of this inflow of reality in order to integrate it into its system and to lower its own level of investment. However, there always remains an element of irreducible otherness. . . . " *Otherness*, 193–94. My concern here is to understand this domain of "too muchness" and irreducible otherness as including a broader sphere of messages and (failed) translation/metabolization.

Freud, for better or worse, called the "death drive" signifies, I want to suggest, this uncanny vitality—this "too much" of pressure—as well as the urge to put an end to it. The *destructive* face of the death drive is thus aimed not at life per se—the natural cycle of growth and decay—but rather at this uncanny, excessive "life" that comes to human being by virtue of its thrownness amidst enigmatic messages.[18]

V

Another way of approaching this important distinction between a merely cognitive and a more properly existential inscription in the realm of social relations is to recall the difference between a "signifier of something" and a "signifier to someone," a difference that became central to the Althusserian conception of the workings of ideology. "What comes to the fore at certain moments," Laplanche writes,

> is that aspect of the signifier which signifies to someone, which interpellates someone, in the sense that we can speak of an official signifying a court decision, or issuing a . . . prefectoral decree. This foregrounding of "signifying to" is extremely important, as a signifier can signify *to* without its addressee necessarily knowing *what* it signifies. We know *that* it signifies, but not what it signifies. . . . Lacan suggests the image of hieroglyphs in the desert, or of cuneiform characters carved on a tablet of stone. . . . It . . . means that the signifier may be *designified*, or lose what it signifies, without thereby losing its power to signify *to*.[19]

What Laplanche is trying to capture here is, I suggest, a distinctly modern notion of *revelation*, perhaps even one that is distinctly Kafkan (of course, once this notion has been elaborated, its

18.   Wagner's operas are obsessed with this excess life. One of the keys to the "Good Friday Spell" in *Parsifal* is undoubtedly its evocation of nature as fully evacuated of this excess life. I am concerned in this book with an alternative—call it a "counter-Wagnerian"—mode of "redemption," as found in the work of Freud and Rosenzweig.

19.   Laplanche, *New Foundations*, 44–45.

effects become visible even in the premodern). At any rate, it was precisely apropos of the status of revelation in Kafka's work that Walter Benjamin and Gershom Scholem discussed the phenomenon of the designified signifier, this peculiar surplus of address over meaning—of, to put it awkwardly, the "*that* it signifies" over the "*what* it signifies"—so central to Kafka's universe. In a now famous letter to Benjamin, Scholem put it this way:

> You ask what I understand by the "nothingness of revelation"? I understand by it a state in which revelation appears to be without meaning, in which it still asserts itself, in which it has *validity* but *no significance* [*in dem sie gilt, aber nicht bedeutet*]. A state in which the wealth of meaning is lost and what is in the process of appearing (for revelation is such a process) still does not disappear, even though it is reduced to the zero point of its own content, so to speak.[20]

It is precisely this "nothingness of revelation," this excess of validity over significance, that so profoundly captures the imagination of the protagonists of Kafka's novels, that becomes, as it were, the most important thing in their lives, the thing from which they are forever struggling to establish a proper distance. As Slavoj Žižek has put it,

> [t]he starting point in Kafka's novels is that of an interpellation: the Kafkaesque subject is interpellated by a mysterious bureaucratic entity (Law, Castle). But this interpellation has a somewhat strange look: it is, so to say, an *interpellation without identification/subjectivation*; it does not offer us a Cause with which to identify—the Kafkaesque subject is the subject desperately seeking a trait with which to identify, he does not understand the meaning of the call of the Other.[21]

The universe of Kafka's protagonists is, in other words, animated by a message that penetrates, even frames, intentional life, a message that in some sense *causes life to matter*, but not in the form

20.   Gershom Scholem, Letter to Benjamin, 20 September 1934, *The Correspondence of Walter Benjamin and Gershom Scholem 1932–1940*, trans. Gary Smith and Andre Lefevre (New York: Schocken, 1989), 142.

21.   Slavoj Žižek, *The Sublime Object of Ideology* (London: Verso, 1989), 44.

of a belief, thought, or meaning; what is at stake is a form of expressivity—"interpellation without identification"—that, in the absence of any propositional content, nonetheless gets under the skin and has some sort of (hindered) revelatory force, has, as Scholem puts it, *validity without meaning*. In psychoanalytic terms, the persistence of validity without meaning (one thinks here of Lear's notion of "*mental* energy without an idea") tells us that a breakdown in meaning—a *trauma*—has left traces in the mind. The mind is left possessed or haunted, under the "ban" of something that profoundly matters without being a full-fledged thought or emotion, that is, anything resembling an orientation in the world.[22] To put it paradoxically, what matters most in a human life may in some sense be one's specific form of *disorientation*, the idiomatic way in which one's approach to and movement through the world is "distorted." The dilemma of the Kafkan subject—exposure to a surplus of validity over meaning—points, in other words, to the fundamental place of fantasy in human life. Fantasy organizes or "binds" this surplus into a schema, a distinctive "torsion" or spin that colors/distorts the shape of our universe, how the world is disclosed to us (Paul Celan spoke of the *Neigungswinkel*, the singular angle of inclination, proper to a human existence).[23] The paradox, however, is that this symptomatic torsion

22. Building on Mikkel Borch-Jacobsen's earlier work on hypnosis, Ruth Leys has, in a recent genealogy of the concept of "trauma," characterized this nonrepresentational aspect of unconscious mental activity, this surplus of validity over meaning at the core of unconscious formations, as the residue of a form of *imitative or mimetic identification* from the prehistory of the subject, that is, from a "time" prior to the distinction between subject and object. For both Borch-Jacobsen and Leys, the upshot of that prehistory, which Freud called "primary repression," is the incorporation into the core of one's own being of a *hypnotic* aspect of the Other's expressivity that henceforth determines the destiny of one's transferences: "prior to the history of the repressed representations of the Oedipus complex, lies a *pre*history of unconscious emotional identifications with or *incorporative bindings to the other;* identifications that precede the distinction between subject and object on which the analysis of desire, even unconscious desire depends." Leys, *Trauma. A Genealogy* (Chicago: University of Chicago Press, 2000), 30–31 (emphasis added). What gets under the skin is, in other words, a fragment of a hypnotic commandment, a sort of somniferous vocal object that gets bound/elaborated in the fundamental fantasy that henceforth frames the course of the subject's desire. It is precisely the "spell" of that hypnotic fragment that concerns both Freud and Rosenzweig.

23. Paul Celan, *Gesammelte Werke* (Frankfurt am Main: Suhrkamp, 1986), 3:168. In a certain sense, psychoanalysis proper begins with the thought that human

is precisely what sustains our sense of the consistency of the world and our place in it: "far from simply deranging/distorting the 'proper balance of things,' fantasy at the same time *grounds* every notion of the balanced Universe: fantasy is not an idiosyncratic excess that deranges cosmic order, but the violent singular excess that *sustains* every notion of such an order."[24]

If fantasy is the means by which we in some sense place ourselves "out of this world," at the "end of the world," it is also a means for securing our adaptation to it. But as I argue throughout this book, both Freud and Rosenzweig conceive of their projects precisely as modes of intervention into this dimension of fantasy and thus into the very thing that at an unconscious level—and often quite rigidly—holds the subject's world together. What is at stake in both projects is the possibility of recovering, of "unbinding," the disruptive core of fantasy and converting it into "more life," the hope and possibility of new possibilities.[25]

VI

In a commentary on Scholem's reading of Kafka, Giorgio Agamben has affirmed Scholem's understanding of the Kafkan universe as one marked by a surplus of validity over significance as the key to the legitimation crisis that defines modernity more generally:

> *Being in force without significance:* nothing better describes the
> ban that our age cannot master than Scholem's formula for

---

beings can suffer not only from this or that inhibition in one's behavior but also from the very way in which the world is disclosed to us from/within our "angle of inclination."

24. Žižek, *The Fragile Absolute*, 86.

25. Because what is primordially repressed has never been a conscious scene, because the impact of an excess of validity over meaning is not itself a delimited and meaningful event/phenomenon, the recovery of traumatic disruption cannot be conceived as a form of memory (of a scene or event). It involves, rather, the opening to a certain meaninglessness or non-sense—an irrationality—at the heart of the repetition compulsions informing one's way of being-in-the-world and therewith the possibility of changing direction in life. We might say that the mode of *verification* of a trauma is not some form of recovered memory—some form of historical *knowledge*—but rather a way of *acknowledging* a distinctive automaticity at the core of one's being.

the status of law in Kafka's novel. . . . Everywhere on earth men live today in the ban of a law and a tradition that are maintained solely as the "zero point" of their own content, and that include men within them in the form if a pure relation of abandonment. All societies and all cultures today . . . have entered into a legitimation crisis in which law (we mean by this term the entire text of tradition in its regulative form, whether the Jewish Torah or the Islamic Sharia, Christian dogma or the profane *nomos*) is in force as the pure "Nothing of Revelation."[26]

For Agamben, the hindered and uncanny nature of revelation in Kafka's universe—the very feature that gives his work its rigorous and, I am tempted to say, pristine, nihilism—merely brings to light what has, in Agamben's view, always belonged to the structure of sovereignty, namely, the moment of *exception*. What is meant thereby— and here Agamben is taking to heart Carl Schmitt's reflections on the state of exception—is that condition in which a sovereign authority suspends the rule of law for the purpose of preserving the life of the state; it is the condition in which sovereign authority continues to be in force while all particular laws and regulations are declared to be suspended. The function of sovereignty itself, Agamben suggests—and here he is following closely Walter Benjamin's notions of "law-making" and "law-preserving" violence—must be seen to include a dimension of immanent traumatism, a point at which the very resources of legitimacy are linked to a power of suspension and disruption. "What is at issue in the sovereign exception," Agamben writes,

> is not so much the control or neutralization of an excess as the creation and definition of the very space in which the juridicopolitical order can have validity. In this sense, the sovereign exception . . . does not limit itself to distinguishing what is inside from what is outside but instead traces a threshold (the state of exception) between the two, on the basis of which outside and inside, the normal situation and chaos, enter into

26. Agamben, *Homo Sacer*, 51.

those complex topological relations that make the validity of
the juridical order possible.[27]

I am proposing that the phenomenon of the transference, both
within individual life as well as collectively, is always structured
around a core of *exposure* to this traumatism, to what we might refer
to as a *meta-juridical* dimension of sovereignty. What is undeadening
in human life is, thus, not exposure to lawlessness as such but rather
to the meta-juridical dimension *of* the law, an exposure that in modernity—and here, Kafka and Freud are among our very best wit-
nesses—in some sense becomes *chronic*. And as Agamben has elsewhere put it, the "Messiah's task becomes all the more difficult from
this perspective. He must confront not simply a law that commands
and forbids but a law that . . . is in force without significance." It is
the situation of "a petrified or paralyzed messianism that, like all
messianism, nullifies the law, but then maintains it as the Nothing
of Revelation in a perpetual and interminable state of exception, 'the
"state of exception" in which we live.'"[28]

Against this background, the man from the country in Kafka's
parable about the law takes on a new, distinctly messianic aspect.
Recalling that in the parable the door-keeper closes the door to the
law that had been, as he finally suggests to the dying petitioner from
the country, destined for him alone, Agamben writes:

27. Ibid., 19. Agamben ends his study with a discussion of the death camps of
Nazi Germany as the site where the state of exception became the rule, the *nomos*, of
political life. He suggests that what the Nazis in effect did was, on the one hand, to *dis-
perse* article 48 of the Weimar constitution across social life in its entirety, while, on
the other hand, concentrating its actual force in the death camps. Article 48 reads as
follows: "The president of the Reich may, in the case of a grave disturbance or threat
to public security and order, make the decisions necessary to reestablish public security, if necessary with the aid of the armed forces. To this end he may provisionally suspend the fundamental rights contained in articles 114, 115, 117, 118, 123, 124, and
153" (cited in ibid., 167). In Nazi Germany, Agamben writes, "*[t]he state of exception . . .
ceases to be referred to as an external and provisional state of factual danger and comes to be con-
fused with juridical rule itself* " (ibid., 168). Agamben's point is that the inmates of the
death camps were the subjects who were most directly exposed to this toxic normaliza-
tion of the state of exception.

28. Agamben, "The Messiah and the Sovereign," in *Potentialities. Collected Essays in Philosophy*, trans. Daniel Heller-Roazen (Stanford: Stanford University Press,
1999), 171. Agamben is alluding here to Benjamin's famous statement on the state of
exception in his *Theses on the Philosophy of History*.

If it is true that the door's very openness constituted . . . the invisible power and specific "force" of the law, then it is possible
to imagine that the entire behavior of the man from the country is nothing other than a complicated and patient strategy to
have the door closed in order to interrupt the law's being in
force.[29]

I suggest that we can more fully grasp and appreciate the messianic
task allegorized in Kafka's parable by seeing it also as an allegory of
a successful analysis, of that passage through the transference that
releases the subject from the always idiosyncratic and *undeadening*
drama of legitimation that had framed its destiny. What calls for
suspension is, in other words, not the law so much as the surplus
excitation that, organized in fantasy, supplements and sustains the
force of juridical normativity in ways that can be paralyzing.

In his essay on Freud with which I began this chapter, Bloom
touches on the concept of undeadness without naming it as such.
There he rather boldly states that the essence of Judaism is the "desire for justice, against the world, and the related inwardness of morality such desire creates." In what we might consider to be a gloss
on Benjamin's difficult notion of "divine violence," Bloom grounds
this claim in his understanding of the outrage at the core of the prophetic dualism that he also links to the Freudian project:

Prophetic dualism is precisely that: Elijah and Amos stand
against the unjust world, and so against all outwardness whatsoever. But this at last is Freud's dualism also: the psyche is at
civil war, but what it wars with, in itself, is the injustice of outwardness, the defensive disorderings of the drives, the unnecessary sufferings that rob us of the freedom that yet can be our
time.[30]

I understand this to mean that both the prophetic tradition and the
Freudian innovation are precisely interventions into the domain of
the undead, the biopolitical "vitality" correlative to our capture by
the sovereign relation, our exposure to its constitutive state of excep-

---

29. Agamben, "Messiah," 174.
30. Bloom, "Freud and Beyond," 154.

tion. The messianic time evoked by Bloom—"the freedom that yet can be our time"—ought then to be thought not so much in terms of a reanimation of the dead—the conventional understanding of the advent of the Kingdom—as of a *deanimation of the undead.* More generally, however, it means that psychoanalysis and theology, the working through of the transference as Freud proposed it and the work on behalf of the Kingdom, as understood within the Judeo-Christian tradition, can and indeed ought to be thought together.

VII

I'd like to end this chapter with a brief coda concerning the notion of enigmatic signifiers. Their efficacy is not limited, as Laplanche at times seems to suggest, to the context of the parent–child relation, though they are clearly most potent, most fateful there. As Scholem's remarks apropos of Kafka's work already suggested, we are always within the "ban" of such signifiers by virtue of the historicity of meaning. We are, that is, always haunted, surrounded by the remainders of lost forms of life, by concepts and signs that had meaning within a form of life that is now gone and so persist, to use Lacan's telling formulation, as "hieroglyphs in the desert." We are thus always, in a certain sense, within the dimension of loss and abandonment. But what is more, we are in the midst of loss we cannot even really name, for when you lose a concept you also lose the capacity to name what has been lost. When, for example, one has lost the capacity to pray, "God," in essence, assumes the status of a designified signifier, a stand-in for an otherwise *nameless loss;* the word signifies, *but not for us* even though we continue, in some sense, to be addressed by it, to live, as Scholem so powerfully phrased it, within the space of its validity beyond and in excess of its meaning.[31]

These dead letters, these "hieroglyphs in the desert," can of

---

31. Against this background, the claim that "God is dead" comes really as something of a relief—a "gentrification" of catastrophe—in that it effectuates a conversion of a far more disturbing, because *nameless,* loss into something we can mourn (I am indebted to Irad Kimhi for this insight). We might characterize the singularity of Friedrich Hölderlin's "poetic courage" as his capacity to truly dwell within this condition, to fully register the impact of the lack of "heilige Namen" *without* thereby positing a death of God.

course become the focus of intense affective charge. What psychoanalysis ultimately tells us is that this is always the case, that our bodies are always haunted by nameless loss, by an ontological incompleteness against which we *defend* by this or that *symptomatic hypercathexis*, by our specific form of "Egyptomania." If there is a "Jewish" dimension to psychoanalytic thought, it is this: the cure is indeed a kind of "exodus," only not one out of Egypt; it offers, rather an exodus out of the various forms of Egyptomania that so profoundly constrain our lives and, while sustaining a level of adaptation, keep us from opening to the midst of life. In the pages that follow I further explore the origins of this Egyptomania as well as the nature of the "therapy" that takes shape at the intersection of Freudian psychoanalysis and Rosenzweig's "new thinking."

CHAPTER THREE

Toward an Ethics of Singularity

I

One of the "canonical" sites where we might fruitfully explore the intersection of psychoanalysis and theology are the memoirs of Judge Daniel Paul Schreber, the Saxon Supreme Court judge made famous by Freud who, in his case study, interpreted the judge's paranoid delusions as fantasmatic elaborations of a homosexual panic. It was, of course, Schreber himself who elaborated his breakdown and partial recovery in theological terms, who grasped, as it were, the psychotheological significance of his crisis. (Schreber, who was aware that his crisis was a crisis of *meaning*, noted, for example, that theologians and philosophers were better prepared to profit from his memoirs than the sort of neurologically and forensically trained psychiatrists who treated him; he intuited, in other words, that what he experienced as physical disorders were ultimately linked to disorders of the mind/spirit and not the brain.) That crisis struck Schreber at a point when he was to assume, by sovereign decree, a position of considerable power and authority in the Saxon judiciary and thus at a time of heightened exposure to the dilemmas pertaining to symbolic investiture (Schreber suffered his psychotic break in conjunction with his nomination to the chair of the highest appellate court in Saxony).

By symbolic investiture I mean, more generally, those social acts, often involving a ritualized transferal of a title and mandate, whereby an individual is endowed with a new social status and role within a shared symbolic universe. It is how one comes into being as—comes to enjoy the predicate/value of—husband, professor, judge, psychoanalyst, and so forth. Within social reality, that is to say, a universe of symbolic relations, one never simply "has" a predicate; whether one likes it or not, whether it is a source of pleasure or not, one's "contraction" of a new predicate has a libidinal component and the rites of symbolic investiture are among the means at a society's disposal for the cultivation and regulation of this "predicative enjoyment."[1] Whatever new status these rites "establish," they do so by combining the two basic meanings of this word. On one level the utterance issued by the Minister of Justice conferring on Schreber the title *Senatspräsident* of the Saxon Court of Appeals merely established, in an official way, the latter's qualifications for the position; it publicly ascertained that Schreber was, as it were, "in himself" already presiding judge. But a symbolic investiture necessarily includes a second level of linguistic effectivity, a more properly performative notion of "establishing," whereby the "in itself" is converted into a "for itself," the attributes of judgeship into the *attribution* of judgeship. Pierre Bourdieu has called this conversion, which adds no fur-

---

1.   With this formulation I am anticipating the Schellingian theory of predication that Rosenzweig adapted in the *Star*. What Schelling, who tries to think together the *logic of predication* and the biblical discourse of *creation/genesis*, means by "contraction" is a kind of withdrawal of the subject into itself, its pure self-positing in the form of negation of all predicative determination, as the "act" presupposed *in* every predication, every *positing* of a predicate of a subject. One of Schelling's analogies for this thought is the drawing of a line. What is presupposed thereby, he argues, is an initial contraction of being to a point, itself understood as the *negation* of the line. See F. W. J. Schelling, *Die Weltalter*, in *Sämtliche Werke*, ed. K. F. A. Schelling (Stuttgart: Cotta, 1856–61), 8:224. In a fine commentary on Schelling's theory of predication, Wolfram Hogrebe offers yet another analogy, that of the runner at the block prior to the start of a race. Before leaping out from the block, the runner, too, in a sense contracts his "being" in order to be able to extend himself out into the space of his activity (running). See Wolfram Hogrebe, *Prädikation und Genesis. Metaphysik als Fundamentalheuristik im Ausgang von Schellings "Die Weltalter"* (Frankfurt am Main: Suhrkamp, 1989).

ther attribute except the absolutely crucial one of title or name, "the principle behind *the performative magic of all acts of institution*."[2]

My reading of Schreber proposes that his experience of what he referred to as "soul murder" and the cosmic disaster associated with it—Schreber's sense that the world had been destroyed, had, in effect, thoroughly ceased to matter, as the result of a profound disturbance in the relation between God and his creation—was grounded in a fundamental impasse in his capacity to metabolize this performative magic, to be inducted into the normative space opened by it. The psychotic's experience of symbolic processes—and above all of language—might thus be understood as a kind of radicalization and literalization of the concept of the *performative* as understood by speech-act theory. A performative utterance is, as J. L. Austin has put it, one that "indicates that the issuing of the utterance is the performing of an action—it is not normally thought of as just saying something."[3] According to one of Austin's more famous examples, then, "When I say, before the registrar or altar, etc., 'I do,' I am not reporting on a marriage: I am indulging in it."[4] For Schreber, *all* speech came to be experienced as the performing of an action and, indeed, as the performing of an ultimately mechanical and nonsensical action *directly on his nerves*. That is, in essence, what "soul murder" signifies: the collapse of the symbolic dimension of even so-called performative speech acts into some form of actual manipulation or influence, some form of direct psychophysical inscription.[5]

2. Pierre Bordieu, *Language and Symbolic Power*, trans. Gino Raymond and Matthew Adamson (Cambridge: Harvard University Press, 1991), 122; emphasis added.

3. J. L. Austin, *How to Do Things with Words* (Cambridge: Harvard University Press, 1975), 6–7.

4. Ibid., 6.

5. A somewhat different way of approaching this concept of "soul murder" is to recall Wittgenstein's remarks concerning the feeling of being guided in one's normative activities, for example, when one adds a set of numbers or draws a line parallel to another one after having been initiated into such activities: "When I look back on the experience I have the feeling that what is essential about it is an 'experience of being influenced' . . . but at the same time I should not be willing to call any experienced phenomenon the 'experience of being influenced'. . . . I should like to say that I had experienced the 'because,' and yet I do not want to call any phenomenon the 'experience of the because.'" Ludwig Wittgenstein, *Philosophical Investigations*, trans. G. E. M. Anscombe (Oxford: Blackwell, 1997), sec. 176. The psychotic, however, is plagued by just

Recalling Harold Bloom's formulation apropos of the conception of authority the benefits of which "ensue from the foundation and augmentation of institutions,"[6] I suggest that Schreber's breakdown was linked to a disturbance in the *transfer* of such benefits. Rather than leading to an expansion and augmentation of symbolic capacities, they precipitated a deranging experience of mental and corporeal intensification. Given the explicitly sexual aspect of this intensification—Schreber felt under divine injunction to cultivate what he referred to as *weibliche Wollust,* feminine *jouissance*—one might say that for Schreber this transfer, this induction into institutional normativity, was experienced as an obscene and never-ending *seduction.* I am arguing, in other words, that this transfer can be understood as a ramification of the processes that Jean Laplanche has analyzed, as we saw in the preceding chapter, as seduction by a message. We might put it this way: a dysfunction or impasse with respect to a *symbolic citation*—Schreber was, at a profound level, unable to recognize himself in the call to be *Senatspräsident*, unable to metabolize his investiture—can return in the form of a *real excitation*. What Schreber discovered is that symbolic investiture includes a kernel of invasiveness, that it can, at least under certain circumstances, introduce into the subject "too much reality."[7]

---

such "experiences of the because." Let us call these "impossible" experiences of a *direct* influence by norms the *specters or spirits*—rather than the *spirit*—of normativity.

6. Harold Bloom, "Freud and Beyond," in *Ruin the Sacred Truths. Poetry and Belief from the Bible to the Present* (Cambridge: Harvard University Press, 1987),160.

7. In his most recent reflections on the impasses of sovereignty, Giorgio Agamben has emphasized the link between our concept of dignity and the processes of symbolic investiture. The concept of dignity, Agamben writes, "has a juridical origin" and refers "to the sphere of public law. Already in the Republican era, the Latin term *dignitas* indicates the rank and authority that inhere in public duties. . . ." *Remnants of Auschwitz. The Witness and the Archive*, trans. Daniel Heller-Roazen (Cambridge: MIT Press, 1999), 66. One still hears this link in the German word for dignity, *Würde*, which immediately suggests the notion of the *Würdenträger,* the bearer of a title or "dignity." Recalling Kantorowicz's study of the theory of sovereignty, Agamben suggests that the enjoyment of dignity, understood as the "substance" generated by symbolic investiture, is correlative to a kind of perpetual animation: "Dignity is emancipated from its bearer and becomes a fictitious person, a kind of mystical body that accompanies the royal body of the magistrate or the emperor, just as Christ's divine person doubles his human body. This emancipation culminates in the principle so often repeated by medieval jurists that 'dignity never dies. . . .'" Ibid., 66–67. I am suggesting—and here I depart from Agamben's project—that in cases of an investiture cri-

These reflections suggest that one might supplement Freud's structural model of the psyche with another topology that I would like to abbreviate as the "Ego and the Ibid."[8] What I mean by this bit of punning is that the *libidinal* component of one's attachment to the predicates securing one's symbolic identity must also be thought of as being "ibidinal": a symbolic investiture not only endows the subject with new predicates; it also calls forth a largely unconscious "citation" of the authority guaranteeing, legitimating one's rightful enjoyment of those predicates (that is at least in part what it means to "internalize" a new symbolic identity). But because that authority is itself in some sense "magical," that is, unsubstantiated, without ultimate foundation in a final ground qua substantive reason, this "ibidity" is, in the final analysis, a citation of lack, and so never settled once and for all.

This "ibidity" could be seen as the psychic registration of the fact that sovereign authority is in some sense grounded in itself, in its own meta-juridical act of self-positing. Indeed, we might even say that this activity is a function of the primordial *ex-citation* of the human subject: its being summoned, called out to engage in a repetitive and interminable citational praxis in relation to a source of authorization that is at some level grounded in itself.[9] Every call to order

---

sis this peculiar animation proper to dignity becomes, in some sense, independent of the title or authority it otherwise sustains. Rainer Maria Rilke's novel, *The Notebooks of Malte Laurids Brigge*, is in large measure a meditation on such crises in the lives of sovereigns as well as in the everyday life of European modernity.

8. Here I am borrowing the title of G. W. Bowersock's review of Anthony Grafton's *The Footnote: A Curious History* (Cambridge: Harvard University Press, 1998), published in the *New Republic*, 19 January 1998.

9. It is, of course, hypnosis that combines the two dimensions I am interested in here, the libidinal as well as the "ibidinal." Hypnosis, which, as Freud insisted, resembles being in love, "coerces" the subject to cite or mime the hypnotist's command. As Mikkel Borch-Jacobsen has put it, "Far from replying to the discourse of the other, the hypnotized person quotes it in the first person, acts it out or repeats it without knowing that he is repeating. He does not submit himself *to* the other, he *becomes the other*, comes to be like the other—who is no longer an other, but 'himself.'" *The Freudian Subject*, trans. Catherine Porter (Stanford: Stanford University Press, 1988), 230.

In an open letter to his psychiatrist, Schreber himself suggested that his breakdown was precipitated by exposure to some sort of hypnotic influence on the part of his doctor: "One might even raise the question whether perhaps all the talk of voices about somebody having committed soul murder can be explained by the souls (rays) deeming it impermissible that a person's nervous system should be influenced by anoth-

addressed to a human subject—and a symbolic investiture is such a call—secretes a "surplus value" of psychic excitation that, as it were, bears the burden, holds the place, of the missing foundation of the institutional authority that issued the call. The fundamental restlessness or unsettledness of the human mind that was of primary concern to Freud and that I earlier characterized as its biopolitical animation is, in large measure, one pertaining to the constitutive uncertainties that plague identity in a universe of symbolic values; due to just such fundamental uncertainties these values are filled with a surplus charge that can never be fully diffused or discharged. It is as if the human psyche always stood in some sort of—albeit historically mutable—relation to the melancholic secret uttered by the chaplain in Kafka's *Trial*. At the end of their long exchange about the possible meanings of the relation between the door-keeper and the man from the country seeking access to the Law, Josef K. expresses perplexed dissatisfaction with the chaplain's point of view:

> "[F]or if one accepts it, one must accept as true everything the doorkeeper says. But you yourself have sufficiently proved how impossible it is to do that." "No," said the priest, "it is not necessary to accept everything as true, one must only accept it as necessary." "A melancholy conclusion," said K.[10]

It is no doubt apropos of such passages that Gershom Scholem, as we saw in chapter 2, formulated his own understanding of the Kafkan universe as one that is permeated by an excess of validity over meaning.

One of the more striking episodes in Schreber's *Memoirs* describes an unnerving epiphany in which just such a surplus—such a

er's to the extent of imprisoning his will power, such as occurs during hypnosis: in order to stress forcefully that this was a malpractice it was called 'soul murder.'" Daniel Paul Schreber, *Memoirs of My Nervous Illness*, trans. Ida Macalpine and Richard A. Hunter (Cambridge: Harvard University Press, 1988), 34–35.

As we shall see, Rosenzweig's understanding of the conception of love opened in Jewish monotheism points precisely to the possibility of intervening into, of loosening the grip of, the hypnotic commandments that have, thanks to the subject's entanglements in processes of symbolic investiture, taken hold of it, generated its specific form of (l)ibidinal "stuckness."

10. Franz Kafka, *The Trial*, trans. Willa and Edwin Muir (New York: Schocken, 1984), 220.

palpable "nothingness of revelation"—impresses itself directly on the mind (Schreber's text as a whole is obsessed with the psycho-physical manifestations of *Unsinn* or nonsense). He describes a night when he encountered, with exceptional force and immediacy, the voices that had been tormenting him (Schreber addresses them with the names of the Zoroastrian deities). It is another scene of investiture and interpellation, one, however, that is closer to a variety of hate speech or curse:

> I believe I may say that at that time and at that time *only*, I saw God's omnipotence in its complete purity. During the night . . . the lower God (Ariman) appeared. The radiant picture of his rays became visible to my inner eye . . . that is to say he was reflected on my inner nervous system. Simultaneously I heard his voice; but it was not a soft whisper—as the talk of the voices always was before and after that time—it resounded in a mighty bass as if directly in front of my bedroom window. The impression was intense, so that anybody not hardened to terrifying miraculous impressions as I was, would have been shaken to the core. Also *what* was spoken did not sound friendly by any means: everything seemed calculated to instill fright and terror into me and the word "wretch" [*Luder*] was frequently heard—an expression quite common in the basic language to denote a human being destined to be destroyed by God and to feel God's power and wrath.[11]

The appellation favored by the deity—*Luder*—has especially rich connotations in the context of Schreber's torments. It can mean wretch, in the sense of a lost and pathetic figure, but can also signify a cunning swindler or scoundrel; a whore, tart, or slut; and finally, the dead, rotting flesh of an animal, especially in the sense of carrion used as bait in hunting. The last two significations capture Schreber's fear of being turned over to others for the purposes of sexual exploitation as well as his anxieties, which would seem to flow from such abuse, about putrefaction, about being left to rot, to suffer the

11. Schreber, *Memoirs*, 124.

fate of abandoned being.[12] What Schreber condenses in this *homo-ludic* epiphany are, I suggest, the effects of coming too close to a surplus of validity over meaning, necessity over truth, that is at some level operative in all institutions that regulate symbolic identities. This surplus is, I want to argue, the very "stuff" of fantasy that is secreted within and by the procedures of investiture, procedures which, in a profound way, inform our relation to possibility and normativity.

To return to the terms suggested by Agamben's reflections on sovereignty, we can say that Schreber experienced, in the form of intense psychic and bodily distress, both sides of the duality comprising the *state of exception:* on the one hand, the sovereign's sanctioned act of suspension of law, which marks a point of indistinction between constituted and constituting power, a point where the validity of sovereign authority—its being in force—outstrips any meaningful content; and on the other hand, the subject's (un)deadening exposure to this zone of indistinction. It is this exposure that bears the potential to transform one into a *Luder* or, as Agamben puts it,

12. We should add to this list of connotations—and here I am indebted to Jerry Flieger's suggestion—the notion of the *ludic*, and thus of Schreber as a kind of *homo ludens.* There is perhaps another possible layer of meaning in the word *Luder*. Schreber may well have known that Martin Luther's family name had been "Luder" before he himself changed it to "Luther" in 1517, the year of his famous ninety-five theses. Before settling on "Luther," he also used a Hellenized form, "Eleutherius," meaning "one who is free." While early enemies of the Reformation made use, in their polemics, of the connotations of putrescence in the name *Luder*, Luther's supporters produced etymologies according to which his name signified "Herr" of the "Leute" ("the people's master") or was derived from the adjective *lauter*, meaning pure, undefiled, genuine. For a comprehensive discussion of Luther's names, see Bernd Moeller and Karl Stackmann, "Luder—Luther—Eleutherius. Erwägungen zu Luthers Namen," in *Nachrichten der Akademie der Wissenschaften in Göttingen. Philologisch-Historische Klasse* 11 (1981): 171–203.

An unconscious identification with the great theological reformer whose own change of name dotted the "i," so to speak, on his radical reshaping of the Christian subject's relation to religious and secular authority, might thus have been operative in Schreber's own experience of spiritual chosenness. In this context one will also recall the bizarre coincidence that the patient on whom Paul Flechsig, Schreber's first psychiatrist, made some of his first neuroanatomical discoveries was a baby named Martin Luther, thereby offering another layer to the overdeterminations of Schreber's "wretched" nomination; to identify with Luther/Luder in this sense would mean to be the "privileged" object of Flechsig's direct and intrusive powers.

a "sacred man," a *homo sacer*.[13] Against this background, one is also able to better appreciate the affinities between Schreber's "conditions contrary to the Order of the World" and the universe of Kafka's writings. Both authors describe the world—or perhaps better, the *protoworld*—from the perspective of "sacred man."[14] What makes Schreber such a powerful witness to these connections is his own insistence on the *generality* of his martyrdom, his profound intuition that the torturous nonsense of the "nothingness of revelation" to which he felt himself exposed was, as Agamben puts it, "the ban that our age cannot master. . . ."[15] For our purposes here, it is crucial to note that Schreber, who was, up until his psychotic break under the maddening pressure of this ban, an utterly nonreligious person, registers his breakdown as a crisis affecting *all* regions of being that in one form or another have traditionally been understood to constitute the *All*: human, divine, worldly. The collapse of the practical unity of life as a space of reason and normative engagement sustained by processes of symbolic investiture—this radical disturbance of Schreber's *being-in-the-world*—abandons Schreber to the pure intensity of undead life, to a protocosmic existence in which all mean-

13.   *"Homo sacer"* signified, according to Agamben, the figure in ancient Roman law deemed unsuitable for sacrifice but who could be killed without punishment. This dual exclusion constitutes the perverse election that inscribes one in the political sphere: "[O]nce brought back to his proper place beyond both penal law and sacrifice, *homo sacer* presents the originary figure of life taken into the sovereign ban and preserves the memory of the originary exclusion through which the political dimension was first constituted. . . . *The sovereign sphere is the sphere in which it is permitted to kill without committing homicide and without celebrating a sacrifice, and sacred life—that is, life that may be killed but not sacrificed—is the life that has been captured in this sphere."* Homo Sacer. Sovereign Power and Bare Life, trans. Daniell Heller-Roazen (Stanford: Stanford University Press, 1998), 83. No doubt the most famous modern literary example of the *homo sacer* is Kafka's Gregor Samsa.

14.   In an essay on Kafka, Walter Benjamin refers to the "protocosmic forces [*die vorweltlichen Gewalten*] which laid claim to Kafka's productivity; forces which one can, to be sure, with just as much right consider to be worldly forces of our own day." "Franz Kafka. Zur zehnten Wiederkehr seines Todestages," in *Benjamin über Kafka*, ed. Herman Schweppenhäuser (Frankfurt am Main: Suhrkamp, 1981), 26–27.

15.   Agamben, *Homo Sacer*, 51. In light of Agamben's reflections on the so-called *Muselmann* in the death camps, one is tempted to think of Schreber's *Memoirs* as the autobiography of someone who had, as it were, touched bottom, had been a sort of *Muselmann*. I am thinking of the catatonic periods early in the illness, the periods when the world had truly disappeared for him.

ingful relations among the regions of being have been effectively supplanted by purely *external* and *nonsensical* ones.

II

I have entered upon this long excursus about Schreber because his case provides a helpful backdrop for what I consider to be one of most important contributions to the complex of issues we have been exploring: Franz Rosenzweig's *The Star of Redemption*. I think that the *Star* can be understood not only as a systematic analysis of those "conditions contrary to the Order of the World" that cost Daniel Paul Schreber his sanity but also as an elaboration of the philosophical and theological resources through which one might open a path beyond them. My claim is that Rosenzweig, too, was ultimately concerned with the various guises of the sovereign exception, with the law that never ceases to secrete its obscene, undeadening supplement through which we all potentially become, though obviously in radically different manners and degrees, *homines sacri*.[16] Indeed, I would go so far as to say that in the *Star*, Schreber, this exemplary modern *homo sacer*, found the philosophically and theologically informed thinker he anticipated in his *Memoirs*. That Rosenzweig would eventually write an explicitly "therapeutic" companion volume to the *Star—Understanding the Sick and the Healthy*—suggests that he himself understood his work as a kind of intervention in the domain of psychopathology, or better: *psychotheology*.[17] As a student of Meinecke and author of *Hegel and the State*, Rosenzweig had, of course, been

16.   In our age, Agamben writes, "all citizens can be said, in a specific but extremely real sense, to appear virtually as *homines sacri*. . . . " *Homo Sacer*, 111. This is so, he adds, "only because the relation of ban has constituted the essential structure of sovereign power from the beginning." Ibid., 111.

17.   See Franz Rosenzweig, *Understanding the Sick and the Health. A View of World, Man, and God*, trans. Nahum Glatzer (Cambridge: Harvard University Press, 1999). As I have already indicated, that book is conceived as a philosophico-theological therapy for metaphysical thinking which is, according to Rosenzweig, precisely the sort of thinking that never emerges from the *protocosmic imaginary*. As I have also suggested, this imaginary assumes a variety of guises; its effectivity is manifest not only in metaphysical thinking but also in the broad spectrum of oedipal fixations that were of primary interest to Freud as well as in the ways in which subjects (fail to) metabolize their experiences of symbolic investiture within this or that institutional context.

steeped in the real and conceptual history of sovereignty. The *Star* carries forward this preoccupation but in terms that have, as it were, fully taken in the catastrophe of the war.[18]

Rosenzweig's discussion of sovereignty largely mirrors Walter Benjamin's better known analysis of "mythical violence" in his short, hermetic essay on the "Critique of Violence" [*Zur Kritik der Gewalt*]. We might even understand Benjamin's essay as a displaced meditation on Schreber's encounter with the force or violence immanent to law, with the "state of exception" internal to the regulation of bodies and identities in society.[19] At the center of Benjamin's reflections is a meditation on a certain self-referentiality of law and legal institutions, which, Benjamin suggests, manifests itself most forcefully in the death penalty. He writes that "in the exercise of violence over life and death more than in any other legal act, *law reaffirms itself.* But in this very violence *something rotten in law* [*etwas Morsches im Recht*] is revealed. . . . "[20] What manifests itself as the law's inner de-

---

18.   Schlomo Avineri has very concisely and compellingly argued that Rosenzweig's entire construction of the meta-historical life of the Jewish people—their life beyond the vicissitudes of the sovereign relation—was motivated by the wartime collapse of Hegelian and Hölderlinian hopes for a state rooted not in force but rather in the rational will of the people, hopes that still permeate *Hegel and the State:* "[T]hat the Hegelian dream turned, despite itself, into the nightmare of 1918, became for Rosenzweig an admonition about the hubris involved in the political kingdom. All those who seek it are doomed to end up in the dialectics of the apotheosis of power and defeat traversed by the German spirit." See Avineri, "Rosenzweig's Hegel Interpretation: Its Relation to the Development of His Jewish Awakening," in *Der Philosoph Franz Rosenzweig (1886–1929)*, ed. Wolfdietrich Schmied-Kowarzik (Munich: Karl Alber Freiberg, 1988), 2:835.

19.   Benjamin writes briefly about Schreber's text in "Bücher von Geisteskranken. Aus meiner Sammlung," in *Gesammelte Schriften*, ed. Rolf Tiedemann, Hermann Schweppenhäuser, and Tillman Rexroth (Frankfurt am Main: Suhrkamp, 1980), 11:615–16. In his biography of Benjamin, Gershom Scholem recalls his friend's participation in a seminar on Freud during his years in Bern for which Benjamin read Schreber's *Memoirs* and wrote a paper about Freud's theory of drives. Scholem remembers that Schreber's book made a more powerful impression on Benjamin than Freud's case study. Benjamin also managed to persuade Scholem to read the *Memoirs*. See Gershom Scholem, *Walter Benjamin. Die Geschichte einer Freundschaft* (Frankfurt am Main: Suhrkamp, 1976), 75.

20.   Benjamin, "Critique of Violence," in *Reflections. Essays, Aphorisms, Autobiographical Writings*, trans. Edmund Jephcott (New York: Schocken, 1986), 286; emphasis added.

cay is the fact that rule of law is, in the final analysis, without ultimate justification or legitimation, that the very space of juridical reason within which the rule of law obtains is established and sustained
by a dimension of force and violence that, as it were, holds the place
of those missing foundations. At its foundation, the rule of law is
sustained not by reason alone but also by the force/violence of a tautological enunciation—"The law is the law!"—which is for Benjamin the source of a chronic institutional disequilibrium and degeneration, of, to use Schreber's term, a sort of chronic *Ludertum*.

Benjamin distinguishes two aspects of this "outlaw" dimension
of law: lawmaking violence [*rechtsetzende Gewalt*] and law-preserving
violence [*rechtserhaltende Gewalt*]. The former refers to the series of
acts that first posits the boundary between what will count as lawful and unlawful; the latter to those acts that serve to maintain and
regulate the borders between lawful and unlawful acts once they
have been established. Benjamin devotes some remarkable passages
to the role of the police in the modern state because they, not unlike
the institution of the death penalty, represent a "kind of spectral
mixture" of these two forms of violence and thus mark "the point
at which the state, whether from impotence or because of the immanent connections within any legal system, *can no longer guarantee
through the legal system* the empirical ends that it desires at any price
to attain." The police is for Benjamin the site where the extralegal
violence upon which the rule of law is structurally dependent is most
clearly manifest. In his evocation of the quasi-demonic aspect of the
police, Benjamin does not shy away from a rhetoric one would be
tempted to call paranoid: "Its power is formless, like its nowhere
tangible, all-pervasive, ghostly presence in the life of civilized states."
He concludes by suggesting that in democratic societies, where the
constitutive role of lawmaking and law-preserving violence is most
fervently disavowed, the open secret of sanctioned police violence
can be especially unnerving:

> And though the police may, in particulars, everywhere appear
> the same, it cannot finally be denied that their spirit is less
> devastating where they represent, in absolute monarchy, the
> power of a ruler in which legislative and executive supremacy

are united, than in democracies where their existence, elevated by no such relation, bears witness to the greatest conceivable degeneration of violence.[21]

As Jacques Derrida has emphasized in a fine commentary on Benjamin's essay, the extralegal dimension of force which it was Benjamin's concern to lay bare to postwar and postrevolution Weimar parliamentarians can be subsumed, as I've suggested in my discussion of the Schreber case, under a more general notion of the performative structure of speech acts.[22] Again, a performative utterance is one that brings about its own propositional content, that establishes a new social fact in the world by virtue of its being enunciated in a specific social context, as when a judge or priest pronounces a couple "husband and wife." Performative utterances are, as a rule, enchained or nested in sets of relations with "lower" levels of performatives that set the stage for their felicitous functioning. Before a judge can perform a marriage ceremony, for example, his effectivity as a social agent must first be established, his symbolic power and authority must first be transferred to him by other performatives that pronounce him "judge." Benjamin's claim is that at a certain point this chain of transferences bottoms out, encounters a missing link at the origin of the symbolic capital circulating through it.[23] To

21. Ibid., 286–87 (emphasis added), 287, 287. No doubt one of the reasons why so many viewers were so transfixed by the videotape of the Rodney King beating some years ago was that it made public the "degeneration of violence" to which African-American men have been chronically exposed in the United States.

22. Jacques Derrida, "Force of Law: The 'Mystical Foundation of Authority,'" in *Deconstruction and the Possibility of Justice*, ed. Drucilla Cornell, Michel Rosenfeld, and David Gray Carlson (New York: Routledge, 1992), 3–67.

23. Much of what Benjamin argues in extremely compact and hermetic prose has been elaborated in a more experience-near idiom by Elaine Scarry in her book *The Body in Pain. The Making and Unmaking of the World* (New York: Oxford University Press, 1985). Scarry's book explores the ways in which, above all in the practices of torture and war, human pain, the "obscenely . . . alive tissue" (31) of the human body, is enlisted as a source of verification and substantiation of the symbolic authority of institutions and the social facts they sponsor. This bottoming out of symbolic function on the body in pain becomes urgent, Scarry argues, when there is a crisis of belief or legitimation in a society: "[A]t particular moments when there is within society a crisis of belief—that is, when some central idea or ideology or cultural construct has ceased to elicit a population's belief either because it is manifestly ficticious or because it has for some reason been divested of ordinary forms of substantiation—the sheer material fac-

those of a "finer sensibility," this missing link is, however, *everywhere* present as, precisely, "something rotten in law."[24] It is, Benjamin suggests, this missing link pertaining to the emergence of institutions that *drives* the symbolic machinery of the law—for Benjamin, the paradigmatic institution—and infuses it with an element of violence and compulsion.

Although he does not evoke the psychoanalytic theory of the drives, Derrida's particular contribution to our understanding of Benjamin's "Critique of Violence" and the "mystical foundation of authority" more generally, is his insistence on the link between performativity and the compulsion to repeat, on the *excitations* correlative to what I have referred to as the *ibidinal* dimension of symbolic identity:

> It belongs to the structure of fundamental violence that it calls for the repetition of itself and founds what ought to be conserved, conservable, promised to heritage and tradition. . . . A foundation is a promise. Every position . . . permits and promises. . . . And even if a promise is not kept in fact, iterability in-

---

tualness of the human body will be borrowed to lend that cultural construct the aura of 'realness' and 'certainty' " (14). One might say that the wounded body is where a society "secretes" what is rotten in law. Speaking more specifically of the structure of war, Scarry argues that "injuring is relied on as a form of legitimation because, though it lacks interior connections to the issues, wounding is able to open up a source of reality that can give the issue force and holding power. That is, the outcome of war has its substantiation not in an absolute inability of the defeated to contest the outcome but in a process of perception that allows extreme attributes of the body to be translated into another language, to be broken away from the body and relocated elsewhere at the very moment that the body itself is disowned . . . "(124). This conception of the injured body as an unspeakable piece of the real that provides the ultimate support of a symbolic order, that (unconsciously) helps to make social facts—governments, money, marriage, social titles, and so on—feel real rather than fictional, allows Scarry, in effect, to recast the psychoanalytic concept of *transference* in more social and political terms. It comes to signify, for Scarry, the "intricacies of the process of transfer that make it possible for the *incontestable reality of the physical body to now become an attribute of an issue that at that moment has no independent reality of its own* . . . " (124–25). What becomes painfully manifest in both war and torture "is the process by which a made world of culture acquires the characteristics of 'reality,' the process of perception that allows invented ideas, beliefs, and made objects to be accepted and entered into as though they had the same ontological status as the naturally given world" (125). We might add that the often spectacular, even theatrical quality of both torture and war underlines the connection to performativity.

24. Benjamin, "Critique of Violence," 286.

scribes the promise as guard in the most irruptive instant of foundation. Thus it inscribes the possibility of repetition at the heart of the originary. . . . Position is already iterability, a call for self-conserving repetition.[25]

III

In the third volume of the *Star*, toward the end of book 1—the one part of the work dealing exclusively with Judaism—Rosenzweig offers, in the context of a larger discussion of "messianic politics," his own highly abbreviated critique of violence in which he emphasizes, above all, the temporality of the "self-conserving repetition" at the heart of sovereignty and the "performativity" proper to it. Rosenzweig characterizes this temporality as *kriegerische Zeitlichkeit*, "time agitated by wars."[26] In existential terms, sovereignty is, for Rosenzweig, a juridico-political "solution" to the problem of positing lasting meaning within and against the forward rush of time. For Rosenzweig, sovereignty is, thus, ultimately a mode of temporalization:

> The world's people as such are without orbits [*Kreislauf*]; their life cascades downhill in a broad stream. If the state is to provide them with eternity, this stream must be halted and dammed up to form a lake. The state must seek to turn into an orbit that pure sequence of time to which the peoples as such are committed. It must transform the constant alternation of their life into preservation and renewal and thus introduce an orbit capable, in itself, of being eternal. (332)

"History," Rosenzweig continues, "seems to fade away in unobstructed alternation and transformation. But the state steps in and imposes its law on the change. Now of a sudden there exists some-

25. Derrida, "Force of Law," 38.

26. Franz Rosenzweig, *Der Stern der Erlösung* (Frankfurt am Main: Suhrkamp, 1990), 368; *The Star of Redemption*, trans. William W. Hallo (Notre Dame: University of Notre Dame Press, 1985), 332. Subsequent references are given in the text and, unless otherwise noted, are to the English translation. The *Star* is composed of three volumes or major parts—Rosenzweig originally wanted to publish them as separate volumes—each divided into an introduction, three "books," and a brief transitional chapter opening to the next stage in the project. The body of the text is organized by numbered sections each of which also has a thematic heading.

thing that endures. Indeed at first sight it now seems as if everything is decreed [*fest-gesetzt*], everything enduring" (332–33). Rosenzweig is playing here, of course, with the German word for law, *Gesetz;* to be *fest-gesetzt* means to be posited, decreed, established as a stable and firm *precedent* that binds the future, which the future is obliged to repeat or iterate. But because of the fundamental tension between law and life, principle and contingency, precedent and novelty, this very process of iteration is internally unstable. Thus, as Rosenzweig puts it, "the state reveals its true face. Law was only its first word. It cannot assert itself against the alternations of life. Now . . . the state speaks its second word: the word of coercion [*Gewalt*]" (333). The repetition of juridical precedent is, in other words, in a quite literal sense the *compulsion to repeat.*[27] It is precisely this dimension of repetition compulsion that defines, for Benjamin, the sphere of "mythical violence" and that Bloom associated with the dynamic of foundation, preservation, and augmentation central to the Roman concept of sovereign power and authority. Again, Rosenzweig's elaboration of this concept emphasizes, above all, its temporal dimension:

> Coercion [*Gewalt*] provides life with legal redress against law. By being coercive itself, and not just legal, the state remains hard on the heels of life. *The point of all coercion is to institute new law.* It is not the denial of law as one might think under the spell of its cataclysmic behavior; on the contrary, it lays the basis for law. But a paradox lurks in the idea of new law. Law is essentially old law. And now it is clear that coercion is: the renewer of old law. In the coercive act, the law constantly becomes new law. And the state is thus equally both lawful and coercive, refuge of the old law and source of the new. . . . At every moment the state is forcibly deciding the contradiction between conservation and renovation, between old law and new. It thus constantly resolves the contradiction, while the course of the people's life only delays the solution perpetually through the onward flow of time. The state attacks the prob-

---

27.   Rosenzweig is no doubt influenced here by Nietzsche's *Genealogy of Morals,* the second essay of which begins with the problem of inducting human beings into a life that includes the concept of *promises,* that is, the notion that the future can be bound by a pledge made in the past.

lem, indeed the *state is itself nothing but the constantly undertaken resolution of this contradiction.* (333; emphasis added)

The consequence of this "being and time" of the state, of its specific mode of "capturing" temporal life, is "that war and revolution is the only reality known to the state; it would cease to be a state the moment where neither the one nor the other were to take place—even if it be only in the form of a thought of war or revolution. The state can at no moment lay down the sword" (333–34). Finally, Rosenzweig characterizes this intervention of sovereign authority into the temporal flow of life—let's call it "sovereign temporalization"—as a form of ban [*Bann*], which can mean, among other things: sovereign authority; the prohibition or punishment decreed by sovereign authority; spell; banishment; abandonment. As Rosenzweig puts it,

> for the new, which otherwise always gets beyond the old, is momentarily confined in its sphere of influence [*Bannbereich*]. It takes the new moment to break the power of the old and to threaten to let life flow on once more as a free river. But at once the state raises its sword again and again condemns the river to a standstill [*bannt den Fluß aufs neue zum Stehenden*], the onward motion to a circle. . . . [I]t is the state which first introduces standstills, stations, epochs into the ceaseless sweep of this life. Epochs are the hours of universal history [*Weltgeschichte*], and only the state introduces them through its martial spell [*seinen kriegerischen Bannspruch*] which makes the sun of time stand still until on any given day "the people shall have prevailed over its enemies." . . . Only the state drops into the current of time those reflections of true eternity which, as epochs, form the building blocks of universal history. (334)[28]

---

28. Both Jean-Luc Nancy and Giorgio Agamben have invoked the concept of the *ban* to characterize the "event" of life's capture by the political, its biopolitical animation/undeadening. In Nancy's words: "To *abandon* is to remit, entrust, or turn over to . . . a sovereign power, and to remit, entrust, or turn over to its *ban*, that is, to its proclaiming, to its convening, and to its sentencing. . . . One always abandons to a law. The destitution of abandoned Being is measured by the limitless severity of the law to which it finds itself exposed. Abandonment does not constitute a subpoena to present oneself before this or that court of law. It is a compulsion to appear absolutely under the law, under the law as such and in its totality. In the same way—it is the same

In a sense, Rosenzweig's theory of the state comes down to a medita-tion on the two meanings of the word *succession*. In its efforts to over-come the meaningless, homogeneous, succession of time, of one moment after the other, the state introduces "standstills, stations, epochs." This mode of overcoming, however, merely transposes the homogeneity of temporal succession into the ceaseless violence of *hegemonic succession:* the succession of empires, rulers, regimes, and ideologies. Though it might appear, in other words, that Rosen-zweig, in contrast to Benjamin, remains attached to a Hegelian vision of universal history, it is clear that this attachment, at least by the time of the composition of the *Star*, had been permeated by a kind of bitter irony.

And indeed, Rosenzweig's ultimate purpose in his reflections on political ontology was to highlight how Judaism and Christianity, in albeit quite different and even antagonistic ways, detach or "un-plug" from this pattern of succession, from the homogeneous course of history defined by it.[29] We might even say that *The Star of Redemp-tion* as a whole, which, I think, holds the key to what Bloom alluded to as "the blessings of more life" (in contrast to "the foundation and

---

thing—to be *banished* amounts not to coming under a provision of the law but rather to coming under the entirety of the law. Turned over to the absolute of the law, the abandoned one is thereby abandoned completely outside its jurisdiction. . . . Abandon-ment respects the law; it cannot do otherwise." Nancy, "Abandoned Being," cited in Agamben, *Homo Sacer*, 58–59.

29.   This gesture of unplugging is the key to Rosenzweig's critique of histori-cism and the false ideology of progress with which it can be associated. That is, with-out a supplementary orientation toward the Kingdom, the historical imagination re-mains stuck in an overly narrow and rigid conception of what is, at any given moment, possible in human society: "The believer in the kingdom uses the term 'progress' only in order to employ the jargon of his time; in reality he means the kingdom. It is the veritable shibboleth for distinguishing him from the authentic devotee of progress whether he does not resist the prospect and duty of anticipating the 'goal' at the very next moment. The future is no future without this anticipation and the inner compul-sion for it, without this 'wish to bring about the Messiah before his time' and the temp-tation to 'coerce the kingdom of God into being'; without these, it is only a past dis-tended endlessly and projected forward. For without such anticipation, the moment is not eternal; it is something that drags itself everlastingly along the long, long trail of time" (227). These lines resonate, of course, with Benjamin's more famous *Theses on the Philosophy of History*. Rosenzweig's point here is that without the intervention of the messianic reference *within* time there is no history proper but only "natural history," that is, the "organic" cycle of the generation and corruption of empires.

augmentation of institutions"), is nothing but an attempt to give a rich philosophical account of this gesture of unplugging as well as of the apparent necessity of its splitting into divergent—Jewish and Christian—modalities or idioms.[30] "Unplugging," as we shall see, need not signify a radical break with social reality, with the rule of a community's law, or even from historical agency; it signifies, above all, a suspension of the haunting, "undead" supplement of the law: a "sabbatical" interruption not of work per se but of a surplus, *fantasmatic labor* at the core of the sovereign relation. One labors, as I have suggested, not only in this or that Egypt but also in the hypercathected fields of one's "Egyptomania" and it is there that the sovereign *Bannspruch*, which is always a *Zuviel von Anspruch*, a "too much of demand," most powerfully captures life, undeadens it, makes it rigid with energy. Recalling Agamben's interpretation of Kafka's parable, "Before the Law," the messianic charge of the man from the country was not so much to bring about an end to Law as such but rather to one's abandonment to its being in force without significance, to the specific configuration of *jouissance* that structures one's psychic capture by Law. The messianic awakening is thus not so much one from our everyday life with the Law as from the "hypnotic" dimension that persists within it, constraining that life and limiting our access to, as Bloom put it, the "freedom that yet can be our time."[31]

---

30. It is, perhaps, in this context that we can understand Walter Benjamin's remark apropos of Robert Walser's characters. They come to us, Benjamin suggests, "from madness and from no place else. They are figures who have brought madness behind them and who therefore manifest such a lacerating, so totally inhuman, imperturbable superficiality. Should one want to name with one word what is gladdening and uncanny about them, one might say: *they are all cured.*" Benjamin goes on to compare the childlike nobility of such convalescents to the figures of fairy tales who, he writes, "also emerge from the night and from madness, that is, from myth." See Benjamin, *Gesammelte Schriften*, ed. Rolf Tiedemann and Hermann Schweppenhäuser, 2:1, 327. It is clear that by "myth" Benjamin means what both he and Rosenzweig characterize as the "protoworld," a world dominated by, under the "ban" of, undeadness. We should note that Benjamin is far less confident that the monotheistic religions have the same capacities as the fairy tale or Walser's stories. Rosenzweig's *Star* is, in its entirety, an effort to demonstrate to people like Benjamin that the biblical traditions continue to be a resource for the emergence from undeadness.

31. Bloom, "Freud and Beyond," 154.

According to Rosenzweig, the possibility of an awakening or exodus—a deanimation of undeadness—is granted with and is, indeed, coterminous with the *event of revelation*. This strange event is understood, in turn, as the intrusion—we might even say violent and disruptive intrusion—into the order of human life of a divine interpellation the content of which is, as Rosenzweig sees it, a demand for love. The key to understanding Rosenzweig's project is to grasp the difference between two kinds of interpellation and their distinctive "objects," to grasp the difference, that is, between *being identified* as a part, as a member of a larger social or political whole— this is the domain sustained by what I have called "symbolic investiture"—and *being singled out* as a part which is no part (of a whole) and which, in Rosenzweig's view, transpires in and through a call of love. . . . These two modes of interpellation are, moreover, fundamentally linked; one can be singled out, Rosenzweig suggests, only on the basis of an impasse within the logic of identification, on the basis, that is, of a symptomatic *remnant* generated by "identificatory" interpellation.[32] To return, once more, to Schreber's idiom, we might say that every symbolic investiture "secretes" a trace element of *Ludertum* manifest as a specific derangement or torsion of one's being, of the habitation of the identity with which one has been invested. For Rosenzweig, revelation—let's call it the language game of divine love—makes it possible to open to as well as intervene in this torsion, to convert a rigidity at the very core of one's being—one that enjoys the double valence of "stuckness" and "animation"—into a resource of transformation.

32. Slavoj Žižek has, I think, this same difference in mind when he distinguishes between the meanings of "subjectivization" in the work of Alain Badiou and Ernesto Laclau, respectively: "[F]or Badiou, subjectivization designates the event of Truth that disrupts the closure of the hegemonic ideological domain and/or the existing social edifice (the Order of Being); while for Laclau, the gesture of subjectivization is the very gesture of establishing a (new) hegemony, and is as such the elementary gesture of ideology." Žižek, *The Ticklish Subject. The Absent Center of Political Ontology* (London: Verso, 1999), 183. One of the great difficulties in Emmanuel Levinas's work is that he in effect has at his disposal only one concept of interpellation, the call to assume responsibility for my neighbor. Because of this, Levinas's characterizations of the ethical summons with regard to the Other often sound like descriptions of a punishing superego. I will return to the problem of the superego in the next chapter.

IV

Before pursuing further the nature of this symptomatic remnant, the conceptualization of which I consider to be one of Rosenzweig's most important achievements in the *Star* (and the one to have received the least scholarly attention), I want to note a crucial aspect of Rosenzweig's understanding of revelation. Since the sovereign relation—the specific way in which it captures life—was largely conceived as a mode of temporalization, it makes sense that revelation will in turn be understood as an intervention into that very temporal achievement. As I have already indicated, there is in Rosenzweig's understanding really only one sort of event that has the power to intervene into "sovereign temporalization," into the time that belongs to the foundation and augmentation of institutions, and that is the fateful advent of love's "divine" imperative. It is, Rosenzweig argues, only the impact of that imperative that opens our eyes to what remains/insists in and beyond the drama of authorization/legitimation.[33] Or rather: the divine imperative is nothing but our opening to this "beyond" that our life in the midst of institutions never ceases to produce. *Rosenzweig's paradox*, if I might call it that, is that our opening to this "beyond" is the very thing that places us in the midst of life, in proximity to our neighbor.

Rosenzweig, however, takes the divinity of this imperative to be something more than a metaphor. If love's imperative is "divine" it is because we are thereby attuned in some sense to a process transpiring *within divinity itself* (or more modestly: where we register a fundamental shift in the concept of divinity and in our life with that concept). Following the trajectory of Schelling's *Weltalter*, Rosenzweig narrates the emergence of the love-imperative out of God's (protocosmic) being as the way in which God's mute eternal essence comes to seize a human life, assumes an urgent eventfulness calling for an impassioned response rather than a posture of contemplation, a relevant mode of *acknowledgment* rather than a claim or pusuit of *knowledge* (in a certain sense, then, this shift signals a passage beyond theology). Rosenzweig's model here is the utterly paradoxical inter-

---

33.   For Rosenzweig, the genre of (ancient) *tragedy* stages the perpetual but hindered opening of this "beyond" *within* the drama of authorization/legitimation.

section of contingency, freedom, and necessity that constitutes the strange event we call "falling in love."[34] To become manifest as something more than mere nature—more, that is, than the substance and structure of positive Being, of *the way things are* and can *be known*, even if we look at them in wonder—God, too, Rosenzweig argues, must be more than a creator; he must also *fall in love* with his creation. Our sense that human life includes a force that exceeds positive Being, that has the capacity not only to inscribe us within but also *to single us out from* the matrix of positive Being is, Rosenzweig suggests, strictly correlative to the advent of divine love (to be singled out is, in this context, something different from being excluded).[35] God reveals himself insofar as he, too, undergoes the vicissitudes of devotion:

> It is the moment which, within its own constricted space, harbors all the weight of destiny, a destiny not "destined" but suddenly there and yet as inescapable in its suddenness as though it were destined from of yore. What is this fate? A glance at that creature which was created in God's image and analogy teaches us the only way we can, the way we must name this intra-divine fate-become-affect. Just as God's caprice, born of the moment, had converted itself into enduring power, so his eternal essence converted itself into—love, a love newly awake with every moment, ever young love, ever first love. For love alone is at once such fateful domination over the heart in which it stirs, and yet so newborn, initially so without a past, so wholly sprung from the moment which it fulfills, and only from that moment. It is wholly compulsion [*ganz Muß*]. . . . From the night of the concealed God, this compulsion bursts forth into the manifest as a Nay, as an ever new self-denial, unconcerned with whatever may have preceded or be yet to

34. Mladen Dolar has written lucidly about this paradoxical intersection of chance and necessity as it is figured in the typical Hollywood melodrama. See his "Beyond Interpellation," in *Qui Parle* 6, no. 2 (spring/summer 1993), esp. 83.

35. We might already note here that in light of this distinction, the Kingdom of God will not be conceived as some sort of final inscription/integration of all subjects into a global totality but rather as the universal arrival of the impact of this dimension of singularity. It will be conceived, in other words, as a form of *universalization* rather than of *globalization*.

come, wholly offspring of the immediately present *coup d'oeil*,
the lived-in moment of life. (160)

What Rosenzweig is aiming at with this rhapsodic, Schellingian speculation is, ultimately, the difference between commandment and law,
Gebot and *Gesetz*. What he describes as an intra-divine event is, in the
end, nothing but the tracing of this difference without which Judaism
would indeed be vulnerable to the charge of being a disciplinary formation demanding mechanical assimilation to a matrix of rules and
ordinances.[36] Reflecting on Deuteronomy 6:5, the commandment to
love God repeated by observant Jews in daily prayer, Rosenzweig
offers a condensed phenomenology of the *temporalization* that takes
place in and through this paradoxical command to love:

> Yes, of course, love cannot be commanded. No third party can
> command it or extort it. No third party can, but the One can.
> The commandment to love can only proceed from the mouth
> of the lover. Only the lover can and does say: love me!—and
> he really does so. In his mouth the commandment to love is
> not a strange commandment; *it is none other than the voice of
> love itself.* (176; emphasis added)

The relevant grammatical distinction regarding this commandment
and its specific mode of temporalization is that between *imperative*
and *indicative:*

36.   Rosenzweig makes this charge with respect to Islam. "'Islam,'" Rosenzweig writes, "is not a condition, a stance of the soul; rather it is an incessant sequence
of obligatory acts. Nor is it the understanding that these obligations are carried out, so
to speak, only symbolically, precisely as sign and visible expression of the pacified condition of the soul or as means to the attainment of this condition. Rather they are esteemed for themselves and indeed they are more or less rational to an extent that pre-
sumably justifies such an esteem. Thus Islam arrives at an explicit ethic of works. Each
individual moral act provides its own yardstick for the measure of resignation to God
required to accomplish it. The harder the deed, the more highly it is esteemed, for the
greater is the resignation to God which is required" (171–72). As is evident from this
passage, Rosenzweig's tendency in the *Star* is, at times, to characterize Islam in some
of the ways in which Judaism had been characterized in nineteenth-century German—
and above all, Lutheran—culture, that is, as a legalistic formation, a religion of pure
heteronomy (perhaps the purest formulation of that view can be found in Otto Wei-
ninger's notorious *Sex and Character*). As we shall see, though, Rosenzweig also embraces several of the worst "charges" made against Judaism in the anti-Semitic dis-
courses of his time.

It ["love me!"] is the imperative becoming audible at the instant of its birth, for emerging and finding voice are one and the same thing in the case of the imperative. The indicative has behind it the whole cumbersome rationalization of materiality, and at its purest therefore appears in the past tense. But "Love me!" is wholly pure and unprepared-for present tense, and not unprepared-for alone, but also unpremeditated. The imperative of the commandment makes no provision for the future; it can only conceive the immediacy of obedience. If it were to think of a future or an Ever [*Immer*], *it would be, not commandment or order, but law.* Law reckons with times, with a future, with duration. The commandment knows only the moment; it awaits the result in the very instant of its promulgation. And if it possesses the magic of the true voice of command, it will truly never be disappointed in this expectation. (177; emphasis added)

Finally, Rosenzweig suggests that the love-imperative has the capacity to draw into its orbit the sovereign temporalization of juridico-political time—the *time of institutions*—which is always structured around the (performative) establishment and iteration of precedents:

Thus the commandment is purely the present. But while every other commandment could equally well have been law if one but viewed it from without and, so to speak, retroactively, the sole commandment of love is simply incapable of being law; it can only be commandment. All other commandments can pour forth their content into the mold of the law as well. This one alone resists recasting; its content tolerates only the one form of the commandment, of the immediate presentness and unity of consciousness, expression, and expectation of fulfillment. For this reason, as the only pure commandment, it is the highest of all commandments, and where it takes the first place as such, there everything else too becomes commandment though otherwise, and viewed from without, it could as well be law. God's first word to the soul that unlocks itself to him is "Love me!" And everything which he may yet reveal to the soul in the form of law therefore without more ado turns

into words which he commands it "today." It turns into execu-
tion of the one initial commandment to love him. . . . It is in
the today that the love of the lover lives, in this imperative today of the commandment. (177)[37]

Before we can fully grasp this crucial distinction between commandment and law—between, to return to Bloom's formulation, the
call that grants the "blessings of more life" and the sovereign acts
that, with explicit or implicit reference to the state of exception,
found and augment institutions (and locate us within them)—we
must first have a better understanding of the *object* of divine love
which I have characterized as a kind of *remnant*. For though Rosenzweig insists on the dynamic of chosenness—love would have no intensity, would not be recognizable *as* love if it lacked this narrowness,
if there were no choice of an object—it is crucial to keep in mind
that this choice does not take place on the basis of any distinguishing
virtues, any special predicates on the part of the object.[38] As I have

37.   In his monograph on Levinas's work, Derrida has underlined another crucial distinction between law and commandment. Law always judges, at least in principle, *in absentia*. A politics left to itself, in other words, left to the order of laws and
universal rules, "would always judge 'in absentia,' always judge only the dead or the absent, where the face is not present, where there is no one to say 'Here I am.'" See
Jacques Derrida, *Adieu. To Emmanuel Levinas*, trans. Pascale-Anne Brault and Michael
Nass (Stanford: Stanford University Press, 1999), 97.

38.   Rosenzweig insists on this "narrowness" to preserve the distinction between a logic of globalization and one of universalization. As he puts it, love never
"proceeds into the breadth of infinity, like an attribute. Though wisdom and power be
omniscience and omnipotence, love is no all-love. Revelation knows of no 'all-loving'
father; God's love is ever wholly of the moment and to the point at which it is directed, and only in the infinity of time does it reach one point after another, step by
step, and inform the All" (164). And further: "As conceived by belief, then, divine love
does not, like light, radiate in all directions as an essential attribute. Rather it transfixes
individuals—men, nations, epochs, things,—in an enigmatic transfixion. It is incalcula-
ble in its transfixion except for the one certainty that it will yet transfix also what has
not yet been transfixed. This would seem to imply a constriction of the concept of divine love, yet this apparent narrow-mindedness first turns this love into veritable love.
Only by hurling itself completely into every instant, even if it be at the cost of forget-
ting all else, only thereby can it really transfix all in the end. . . . A love which had
transfixed all from the first would . . . simply be a From-the-first, only a past. It would
not be that which first makes love constitute love: the present; pure, unadulterated
present" (164–65). A corollary of this view is that *failure* on the part of the love-
object—the beloved—will not be understood as a failure *to be* something or other but
rather as a failure *to respond*.

indicated already, divine love in Rosenzweig's view is nothing but the opening up of possibilities of facing up to—of in some sense "countenancing"—that in the subject which is "more" than the subject, the "too much" of pressure, the excess of reality that is, in large measure, organized in the fantasies that bind us to social reality.

V

In the *Urzelle* or "Germ Cell" of the *Star,* Rosenzweig already laid out, in the "mathematical" notation he would later adapt in the *Star,* his basic conception of such a remnant. Here as in the *Star,* Rosenzweig's "new thinking," that is, his break with the philosophical systems of German Idealism and metaphysical thinking more generally, emerges with the notion of the extra- or meta-ethical "insistence" of the human subject. This is the notion of a dimension of human being that can never be consumed by any kind of generality, whether in the form of a concept, cause, or other kind of identification:

> After it [philosophical Reason] has taken everything into itself and proclaimed its exclusive existence, the human being suddenly discovers that he, who has after all long been digested philosophically, *is still there.* . . . I, the quite ordinary private subject, I first and last name, I dust and ashes, I am still there. And I philosophize, that is: I have the gall to philosophize the sovereign ruler Philosophy.[39]

The *Star* reiterates this anti- or counterphilosophical gesture and links it directly to the ultimate recalcitrance of human mortality, to death's irreducible, non-metabolizable facticity that figures, in Rosenzweig's thought, as the ultimate source-object of the drive:

> [A]nd truthfully death is not . . . Nought [*Nichts*], but a something from which there is no appeal, which is not to be done away with. Its hard summons sounds unbroken even out of the mist with which philosophy envelops it. Philosophy might well have swallowed it up into the night of the Nought, but it

39.   "'Germ Cell' of the *Star of Redemption,*" in *Franz Rosenzweig's "New Thinking,"* ed. and trans. Alan Udoff and Barbara E. Galli (Syracuse: Syracuse University Press, 1999), 48; emphasis added.

could not tear loose its poisonous sting. And man's terror [*Angst*] as he trembles before this sting ever condemns the compassionate lie of philosophy as cruel lying. (4–5)[40]

For Rosenzweig, what accounts for the singularity of a human existence, what ultimately makes a human life irreplaceable, is not this or that positive attribute—some determinate *predicate*—but rather the utter alterity of death which installs in life a fundamental nonrelationality, a dense core of existential loneliness that in some sense *is* who we are. "Only the singular can die and everything mortal is solitary." It is, in a word, death that separates out, that "distinguishes the singular from the All" (4). To "count" as singular one has to be, as it were, *supernumerary*, to persist beyond the logic of parts and wholes, beyond cultural systems of exchange, distinguished not by this or that trait but rather by *being left over*, by *remaining* once all particularities have been accounted for. It is death that first endows existence with this kind of singular density, with what Rosenzweig characterizes as an *"unverdauliche Tatsächlichkeit,"* an "indigestible actuality outside of the great intellectually mastered factual wealth of the cognitive world" (11).

In the third book of the first volume of the *Star*, Rosenzweig more fully develops this thought of what I'd like to refer to as *death-driven singularity* under the heading of the *"metaethical self,"* which he distinguishes from the concept of the "personality." The personality signifies what is *generic* about a person, that is, everything about a person that can be subsumed under a concept, that can be subordinated to some sort of universal or genus. For Rosenzweig, the paradigm of this subsumption is progeniture: "Natural birth was . . . the birth of individuality; in progeniture it died its way back into the genus" (70). Rosenzweig abbreviates this subsumption by the equa-

---

40.   The *Star*, some of which was composed in the Balkans where Rosenzweig was assigned to an anti-aircraft unit during World War I, begins with an evocation of the trenches as the ultimate counterargument to metaphysics: "Why should philosophy be concerned if the fear of death knows nothing of such a dichotomy between body and soul, if it roars Me! Me! Me! . . . Let man creep like a worm into the folds of the naked earth before the fast-approaching volleys of a blind death from which there is no appeal. . . " (3). In the *Star*, Rosenzweig also identifies his most important philosophical precursors in these efforts to open thinking to the impact of human finitude: Schopenhauer, Kierkegaard, and Nietzsche; their work resonates throughout the *Star*.

tion $B = A$, signifying the entrance of what is particular, individual, distinctive [*das Besondere*] into the general or universal [*das Allgemeine*]:

> Many predications are possible about personality, as many as about individuality. As individual predications they all follow the scheme $B = A$, the scheme in which *all the predications about the world and its parts* are conceptualized. Personality is always defined as an individual in its relation to other individuals and to a Universal. (69; emphasis added)

But as he quickly adds, "There are no derivative predications about the self, only the one, original $B = B$" (69). The self, that is, signifies *the part that is no part* (of a whole), a nonrelational excess that is out of joint with respect to the generality of any classification or identification.

To put it in the most mundane terms, when one reads "personal ads" in the newspaper, one typically finds listings of the positive attributes someone is searching for in a partner: stable professional life, loves travel, sushi, long walks on the beach, and so on. All such attributes belong to the *personality:* any number of people can fit the bill, no one is truly singled out by these generic properties, and any number of other people might identify with the list as the résumé of the kind of partner they would want. We are, in a word, within the order of exchange and substitution, the order of $B = A$ (the typical abbreviations used in personal ads—"SWF"—underline the generality of the "object" being addressed). But as we all know—and here we touch on the truth of what might at first glance look like mere sentimentality—when one truly loves another person, one loves precisely what is *not* generic about them, what cannot be substituted for by someone else, in a word, what is irreplaceable. But this singular "something" that Rosenzweig calls the (metaethical) self and that resists generic identification—that has no general equivalent—is not some other, more substantial self behind the personality, not, that is, some sort of true self that, say, assumes a distance to the social roles of the personality; it is, rather, a *gap* in the series of identifications that constitute it. Borrowing the discourse of the infinitesimal calculus, Rosenzweig at times refers to this gap that nonetheless manifests a peculiar positivity as a *differential.* To paraphrase Scholem's formulation apropos of Kafka (and Jonathan Lear's on mental energy), we might understand the self as a limit concept of the personality, as the *personality at the zero-point of its (predicative) content.* One might think here, too, of Roland Barthes's distinction between the *studium* and *punctum* of a photograph. By "studium" Barthes means

> a kind of general, enthusiastic commitment . . . but without special acuity. It is by *studium* that I am interested in so many photographs, whether I receive them as political testimony or enjoy them as good historical scenes: for it is culturally (this connotation is present in *studium*) that I participate in the figures, the faces, the gestures, the settings, the actions. . . . The second element will break (or punctuate) the *studium*. This time it is not I who seek it out (as I invest the field of the *studium* with my sovereign consciousness), it is this element which rises from the scene, shoots out of it like an arrow, and pierces me.[41]

The *punctum* is not an intervention of another order of reality, but a rising to consciousness of a non-symbolizable surplus within an otherwise intelligible reality, a sort of stain on the horizon of cultural intelligibility. When we are touched by the punctum of a photograph, we have been touched by a remainder, something leftover from our "reading" of the studium. It was precisely this distinction that led Rosenzweig to characterize the methodology of the *Star* as "absolute empiricism," as openness to this *surplus of the real within reality.*[42] As Emmanuel Levinas has put it, what is at stake in the metaethical self—the $B = B$—is the "surplus of being, this existential exaggeration that is called *being me*—this protrusion of ipseity into being. . . . "[43]

41. Roland Barthes, *Camera Lucida. Reflections on Photography*, trans. Richard Howard (New York: Hill and Wang, 1981), 26.

42. Rosenzweig coins the term *absolute empiricism* in "The New Thinking." See Rosenzweig, *New Thinking*, 101.

43. Emmanuel Levinas, *Basic Philosophical Writings*, ed. Adriaan Peperzak, Simon Critchley, and Robert Bernascoin (Bloomington: Indiana University Press, 1996), 17. For Levinas, this "protrusion" is "accomplished as a turgescence of responsibility" (17). For Rosenzweig, it is responsibility born in love that brings to light, makes mani-

VI

Yet another way of thinking of the distinction between the personality and the self is with reference to the concept of *teleology*. The formula correlative to personality, $B = A$, can be understood as an instance of teleological subsumption: some particular, distinctive feature is taken up into a larger purpose, finds its place within a teleologically structured whole. Our predicates provide an index of our participation in, our absorption by, such wholes. From the perspective of the personality, every individual ("B") is the basis of a teleological judgment, an evaluation of its *goodness for* some higher purpose ("A"). Against the background of the personality, the self signifies a break with teleology; the self is, in a fundamental sense, *good for nothing*, a rupture in the very logic of teleological evaluation. Rosenzweig thereby underlines a paradox pertaining to man's place in the "chain of being." Man is a being distinguished by his sensitivity to teleology, that is, a capacity to appreciate teleology in nature—even if generated by the blind dynamic of natural selection—as well as by his ability to think teleologically with respect to his own being, to make plans, to organize his activities in purposeful ways. But he is, at the same time, the being who most radically breaks with teleology, who is capable of utterly purposeless activity. As Slavoj Žižek has put it apropos of Schelling's conception of the Fall:

> Therein resides the ultimate paradox of teleology: it is easy to discover hidden Purposes in nature, which acts blindly, as a purposeless mechanism; whereas man—who, in his activity, consciously pursues goals—gets involved in a meaningless expenditure of his potential. . . . Man hampers the free circulation of nature, he is a kind of embolism in the upward flow of natural energies. . . . [44]

Because the self pertains to that which in some sense persists beyond an individual's teleological integration into the life of the

---

fest, an ipseity that is in some "protocosmic"—and often tragic—sense always already there.

44.   Slavoj Žižek, *The Indivisible Remainder. An Essay on Schelling and Related Matters* (London: Verso, 1996), 58.

genus, "we should," Rosenzweig writes, "be led to the inadequacy of the ideas of individuality and personality for comprehending human life" (70–71). Rosenzweig circumscribes what remains/insists beyond these ideas by means of the concepts of *character* and *defiance;* the self signifies nothing but the defiant persistence of one's character, its *demonic self-sameness.* This is what Rosenzweig tries to capture by the tautology, *B = B:* a distinctive insistence on pure distinctiveness.[45] This leads him to the thought of the second birth and second death as constitutive features of human existence (one hears in this passage the resonances of Rosenzweig's letter to Meinecke, described in chapter 1, in which he distinguished between the rule of his academic talents and the "dark drive" that interrupted their dominance):

> Character, and therefore the self which bases itself on it, is not
> the talent which the celestials placed in the crib of the young
> citizen of the earth "already at birth" as his share of the com-
> monweal of mankind [*am gemeinsamen Menschheitsgut*]. Quite
> the contrary: the day of the natural birth is the great day of
> destiny for individuality, because on it the fate of the distinc-
> tive [*das Schicksal des Besonderen*] is determined by the share in
> the universal [*den Anteil am Allgemeinen*]; for the self, this day
> is covered in darkness. The birthday of the self is not the same
> as the birthday of the personality. For the self, the character,
> too, has its birthday: one day it is there. It is not true that char-
> acter "becomes," that it "forms." One day it assaults man like
> an armed man and takes possession of all the wealth of his
> property. . . . Until that day, man is a piece of the world even

45. "True, ethos is content for this self and the self is the character. But it is not defined by this its content; it is not the self by virtue of the fact that it is this particular character. Rather it is already self by virtue of the fact that it has a character, any character, at all. Thus personality is personality by virtue of its firm interconnection with a definite individuality, but the self is self merely by its holding fast to its character at all. In other words, the self 'has' its character" (72). In his commentary on Schelling's *Weltalter,* the most important philosophical precursor to Rosenzweig's project, Žižek puts it this way: "That which, in me, resists the blissful submergence in the Good is . . . not my inert biological nature but the very kernel of my *spiritual* selfhood, the awareness that, beyond all particular physical and psychical features, I am 'me,' a unique *person,* an absolutely singular point of spiritual self-reference." Žižek, *Invisible Remainder,* 59.

before his own consciousness. . . . The self breaks in and at one blow robs him of all the goods and chattel which he presumed to possess. He becomes quite poor, has only himself, knows only himself, is known to no one, for no one exists by he. The self is solitary man in the hardest sense of the word: the personality is the "political animal." (71)[46]

And as Rosenzweig indicates, the "birth" of the metaethical self is correlative to what Freud characterized as the emergence of *Triebschicksal*, the drive-destiny that distinguishes human existence from other creaturely life. In his most explicit characterization of the death-driven singularity of the self, Rosenzweig writes:

Thus the self is born on a definite day. . . . It is the day on which the personality, the individual, dies the death of entering the genus [that is, in progeniture]. . . . This speechless, sightless, introverted *daimon* assaults man first in the guise of *Eros*, and thence accompanies him through life until the moment when he removes his disguise and reveals himself as *Thanatos*. This is the second, and, if you will, the more secret birthday of the self, just as it is the second, and, if you will, the first patent day of death for individuality. . . . Whatever of the self becomes visible to us lies between these two births of the *daimon*. (71–72)[47]

46. Robert Musil's early novel, *The Confusions of Young Törless*, is no doubt one of the most compelling accounts of this "birthday" of the metaethical self. One of Törless's achievements in the novel is his refusal to subscribe to the metaphysical understanding of this emergent self—its positing as some sort of substantial or cosmic soulthing—elaborated by his school friend Beineberg.

47. Here we might recall Borch-Jacobsen's remarks concerning the hypnotic-mimetic dimension of the "event" of primary repression which is, in essence, the formation of the metaethical self under the impact of the Other's seductive enigma (Borch-Jacobsen's notion of hypnosis is, I am suggesting, another version of Laplanche's conception of seduction): "[H]ypnosis involves the birth of the subject—perhaps not a repetition of the birth event, but birth as repetition, or as primal identification: in it the subject comes into being (always anew: this birth is constantly repeated) as an echo or duplicate of the other, in a sort of lag with respect to its own origin and identity." The Other, understood here as hypnotic agency, "*destines* his receiver or *destinataire:* he determines him in his most proper being, gives him his own selfhood even as he withholds himself in that donation." Borch-Jacobsen, *Freudian Subject*, 231, 230. The metaethical self, this bit of addiction to the Other's enigma, is, we might thus say, an index of a hypnotic rapport at the basis of at least certain structures

Between two births, between two deaths: such is the uncanny locus of the self. And as Rosenzweig adds, this space between two births/deaths constitutes the strange state of immortality—of insistence—that I have characterized as undeadness. Thus, concerning the hero of Attic tragedy who, in his view, first gives visible shape and historical urgency to this metaethical self, Rosenzweig writes, "the tragic hero does not actually die after all. Death only cuts him off, as it were, from the temporal features of individuality. Character transmitted into heroic self is immortal" (79). And with immortality, Rosenzweig continues,

> we touch on an ultimate yearning of the self. Personality does not demand immortality for itself, but the self does. Personality is satisfied with the eternity of the relations into which it enters and in which it is absorbed. *The self has no relations*, cannot enter into any, remains ever itself. Thus it is conscious of being eternal; *its immortality amounts to an inability to die.* All ancient doctrines of immortality come down to this inability of the disengaged self to die. Theoretically, the only difficulty consists in finding a natural bearer of this inability to die, a "something" that cannot die. (79; emphasis added)

Rosenzweig's language apropos of the metaethical self can help clarify a crucial development in Freud's theory of the drives. As is well known, Freud's theory moved from an initial dualism, that of the ego drives and the sexual drives, which he at times characterized as a distinction between drives of *self*-preservation and drives of *species*-preservation, to the infamous dualism first introduced in *Beyond the Pleasure Principle* and to which he remained committed to the end, namely, that of the death/destruction drives and the erotic or life drives. Rosenzweig's discussion of the self leads us to the thought, however, that Freud's revision was made necessary by a misunderstanding of the concept of the self relevant to the drives of

---

of intersubjective and institutional relations. In some sense, then, we get a foothold in Being on the basis of a kind of hypnotic suggestion/seduction, but one—and here is where the concept of hypnosis can be misleading—that for the most part emanates from the Other's *unconscious*. What Rosenzweig as well as Freud are ultimately interested in are ways of intervening into these fateful and hypnotic remnants, in essence, of awakening the *destinataire* to the possibility of a genuine shift of direction.

self-preservation. In his later lectures, Freud notes, for example, that these drives lack the plasticity and mobility of the libido, that they are "implacable, resistant to deferral," that they "are *imperative in a totally different way*" than sexual drives which are famously susceptible to the primary processes.[48] But because Freud linked the distinctive implacability of the drives of self-preservation to purely biological imperatives of survival—thirst and hunger—he was forced to posit a different and darker source of psychic rigidity once he began to confront the phenomenon of repetition compulsion. It was this darker source that he identified as the death drive. Rosenzweig's conception of the metaethical self would seem, however, to make this further step unnecessary by collapsing the distinction between the ego drives and the death drive. Once we understand the self as the metaethical self, *self*-preservation can, of course, include the gesture of *refusing* food and water (certainly any parent confronting a child's capacity for utter, demonic defiance in the face of parental solicitude and concern for its "good," has an intuitive grasp of metaethical selfhood.) [49]

Again, we might put it in the term's of the love relation. In thinking about the beloved, the lover's mind opens upon an infinite series of predicative determinations: B (my beloved in his/her particularity) $= A_1, A_2, A_3, A_4$. . . . The *predicative being* of the beloved is

48.   Freud, *Neue Folge der Vorlesungen zur Einführung in die Psychoanalyse*, in *Studienausgabe* (Frankfurt am Main: Fischer, 1982), 1:531 (lecture 32); emphasis added.

49.   Kant had already adumbrated this other sense of self-preservation in his discussion of the sublime in the *Critique of Judgement:* "In the same way, though the irresistibility of nature's might makes us, considered as natural beings, recognize our physical impotence, it reveals in us at the same time an ability to judge ourselves independent of nature, and reveals in us a superiority over nature that is the basis of *a self-preservation quite different in kind from the one that can be assailed and endangered by nature outside us*." *Critique of Judgement*, trans. Werner S. Pluhar (Indianapolis: Hackett, 1987), 121; emphasis added. This "sublime" conception of self-preservation is at the heart of a semantic difficulty in Schelling's thought which runs through the *Weltalter* fragment that so deeply influenced the *Star*. Schelling, too, is trying there to elaborate a conception of the self—he speaks of "*Selbstheit*" and "*Egoität*," selfhood and egoity— which is strictly *opposed* to identity, that is, a notion of the self as a *barring* of its identification, as a defiant *repulsion* of all predicative determination. Because what we commonly refer to as the ego is essentially a bundle of identifications, Schelling's notion of "egoity" is paradoxically that of a radically *counter-egoic* force, really more a notion of *Nicht-Ich* than of *Ich* or ego. And again, it was no doubt the discovery of this radical *negativity* proper to the self that led Freud to posit the death drive.

without limit, an infinitely expanding field of metonymic displacements. We might say that the elaboration of the predicative being—the "Whatness"—of the Other, functions according to the pleasure principle: each predicate "discharges" some of the tension sustaining my efforts to locate the essence of the beloved. But at the very heart of these efforts there is the "pulse" of an encounter with the Other in his or her sheer, "tautological" presence—his or her "ipseity"—beyond predicative being, beyond the "whatness" of essences. In the *Project*, the term Freud uses to capture this tautological kernel of the Other—his or her "*B = B*"—is *Thing* (*das Ding*). Speaking of the perceptual experience of another human being—"*ein Nebenmensch*," the human being next to me, my neighbor—Freud writes: "And so the complex of the neighbor divides into two constituent parts the first of which *impresses* [*imponiert*] through the constancy of its composition [*durch konstantes Gefüge*], its persistence as a *Thing* [*Ding*], while the other is *understood* by means of memory-work. . . . "[50]

We might say that Rosenzweig's entire philosophico-theological project is dedicated to showing how the biblical conceptions of revelation and redemption take up this uncanny, metaethical kernel of human existence—this peculiar surplus of *insistence* over *existence*—without thereby positing a substantial something as its thing-like bearer. Indeed, Rosenzweig's whole point is that the self is *not* a thing—not even a noumenal Thing—but rather a tautological point of self-reference opening a breach in the chain of being. A corollary of this view, however, is the paradox—and this is no doubt what Freud was getting at when he spoke of the neighbor qua Thing—that only another human self, that is, only a non-thing-like, *spiritual* being, truly enjoys the opaque density we usually associate with *matter*, with *being a thing*. In this sense, Rosenzweig is a sort of historical materialist, a thinker for whom history—or, perhaps better, "historicity"—is ultimately concerned with the destiny of this peculiar materiality of human selfhood. Rosenzweig's understanding of the notion of love central to the biblical traditions—love of neighbor—will thus have to be framed as an encounter with one's neighbor *in his or her death-driven singularity*, as an encounter, that is, with my

50. Freud, *Gesammelte Werke, Nachtragsband: Texte aus den Jahren 1885–1938* (Frankfurt am Main: Fischer, 1987), 426–27.

"neighbor-Thing." As Slavoj Žižek has put it in his psychoanalytic commentary on Schelling's *Weltalter*-fragment,

> when do I effectively encounter the Other "beyond the wall of language," in the real of his or her being? Not when I am able to describe her, not even when I learn her values, dreams, and so on, but only when I encounter the Other in her moment of *jouissance:* when I discern in her a tiny detail—a compulsive gesture, an excessive facial expression, a tic—that signals the intensity of the real of *jouissance.* This encounter of the real is always traumatic, there is something at least minimally obscene about it, I cannot simply integrate it into my universe, there is always a gap separating me from it.[51]

VII

To bring these reflections to a provisional conclusion, what both Rosenzweig and Freud give us to think is that the very locus of our psychic rigidity—what I have referred to as our biopolitical animation or undeadness—at the same time harbors our singular resource for "unplugging" from our capture by the sovereign relation. The very dynamic that attaches us to an ideological formation is, in this view, the site where the possibility of genuinely new possibilities can emerge. Our symptom, the very thing that impedes life, constrains our movement in the world, is at the same time the source of what Bloom referred to as the "blessings of more life." In Hölderlin's famous words, "Yet where danger lies, / Grows that which saves."[52] But more than that, both Freud and Rosenzweig suggest that being-in-the-midst-of-life means being with another subject in the singularity of his or her *jouissance*, his or her "Egyptomania." It means exposure

---

51. Slavoj Žižek, "The Abyss of Freedom," in *The Abyss of Freedom/Ages of the World* (Ann Arbor: University of Michigan Press, 1997), 25. Žižek's formulation is, of course, based not on Rosenzweig but rather on the "ethics of psychoanalysis" adumbrated by Lacan's reading of the notion of the *Thing* in Freud. See *The Seminar of Jacques Lacan. Book VII. The Ethics of Psychoanalysis*, trans. Dennis Porter (New York: W. W. Norton, 1992).

52. The lines come from the first strophe of Hölderlin's hymn, "Patmos." See *Hymns and Fragments by Friedrich Hölderlin*, trans. Richard Sieburth (Princeton: Princeton University Press, 1984), 89.

not simply to the thoughts, values, hopes, and memories of the Other, but also to the Other's touch of madness, to the way in which the Other is disoriented in the world, destitute, divested of an identity that firmly locates him or her in a delimited whole of some sort (as I have been arguing, this very destitution often gives our *attachments to* existing social reality their specific urgency and compulsiveness). It means exposure to the insistent expressivity that Freud linked not to human consciousness, to the nature of intentionality, but rather to the symptomatic agency that constitutes the real subject of psychoanalysis—let's call it the *dreaming subject.* What Freud and Rosenzweig have done, then, is to elaborate the ethical relation introduced into the world by Judeo-Christian monotheism—love of God *as* love of neighbor—as the basis of a distinctly modern ethical conception: my obligation to endure the proximity of the Other in their "moment of *jouissance,*" the demonic and undying singularity of their metaethical selfhood (in Freud's view, it is perhaps only *psychoanalysts* who—at least ideally—embody this ethical attitude). To put it most simply, the Other to whom I am answerable *has an unconscious,* is the bearer of an irreducible and internal otherness, a locus of animation that belongs to no form of life. To cite Freud's famous characterization of the Ratman, the face of the Other to whom I am answerable is one that in some form or another manifests a *"horror at pleasure of his own of which he himself [is] unaware."*[53]

As I argue in chapter 4, this internal otherness needs to be analyzed with reference to the psychic agency that Freud called the *superego.* In his various remarks concerning the superego, Laplanche has himself suggested that the genesis of this peculiar agency be understood within the framework of an especially virulent modality of seduction by the enigmatic message. Concerning Kant's moral philosophy, for example, Laplanche writes:

> There are good grounds for looking very seriously into the notion that the categorical imperative is born of the superego, and for dwelling on one specific aspect of it: categorical imperatives cannot be justified; they are certainly enigmatic in the

53. Freud, *Notes upon a Case of Obsessional Neurosis,* in *The Standard Edition of the Complete Psychological Works,* ed. and trans. James Strachey (London: Hogarth Press, 1953–74), 10:166–67.

same way that other adult messages are enigmatic; but not only are they unjustified, it is possible that they are unjustifiable, or in other words non-metabolizable. This means that they cannot be diluted, and cannot be replaced by anything else. They exist, and they are immutable and cannot by symbolized. They resist the schema for the substitution of signifiers.[54]

Laplanche refers to such non-metabolizable remainders as "psychotic enclaves inside the human personality as such. . . . "[55] And as he puts it in a later essay where he distinguishes between the "implantation" and the "intromission" of an enigmatic message:

> Implantation is a process which is common, everyday, normal or neurotic. Beside it, as its violent variant, a place must be given to *intromission*. While implantation allows the individual to take things up actively, at once translating and repressing, one must try to conceive of a process which blocks this, short-circuits the differentiation of the agencies in the process of their formation, and puts into the interior an element resistant to all metabolization. . . . I have no doubt that a process related to intromission also has its role in the formation of the *superego*, a foreign body that cannot be metabolized.[56]

I would suggest, instead, that we think of the superego as the psychic agency that sponsors a minimal *organization* or binding of the metaethical surplus into a kind of (albeit hindered) ethics or behavioral *Gestalt*, that is, that "principled" form of suffering that we characterize as a neurosis of one kind or another. Under the aegis of the superego, we are, as it were, free to suffer in one recognizable way or another rather than more directly register the metaethical insistence at the heart of the personality. Or rather, the superego *is* the metaethical self conceived as a determinate failure or limitation of some sort—the failure to be a part of a whole—that could be and ought

---

54. Jean Laplanche, *New Foundations for Psychoanalysis*, trans. David Macey (Oxford: Basil Blackwell, 1989), 138–39.

55. Ibid., 139.

56. Jean Laplanche, *Essays on Otherness* (London: Routledge, 1999), 136.

to be remedied.[57] Using Rosenzweig's "calculus," we might formulate the capricious demands of the superego as so many versions of the (impossible) equation or "mathematical" law: $(B = B) = A$. It is my claim in this book that both Freud and Rosenzweig help us to understand what it means to intervene into this superegoic structure that would seem to form the deepest kernel of our psychic inertia and "stuckness." Indeed, as I shall argue, the redemption at stake in the *Star of Redemption* is, in a crucial sense, nothing but the way we make it possible for our neighbor to convert the *ban of superego* into the "blessings of more life."

It is in this spirit that I understand the emphasis Rosenzweig places on the emotion of *shame*—rather than guilt—with respect to at least a certain kind of sin: the sin of lovelessness which, in its turn, only becomes manifest in the light of love:

> But it is hard to admit that one was without love in the past. And yet—love would not be the moving, the gripping, the searing experience that it is if the moved, gripped, seared soul were not conscious of the fact that up to this moment it had not been moved nor gripped. Thus a shock [*eine Erschütterung*] was necessary before the self could become beloved soul. And the soul is ashamed of its former self, and that it did not, under its own power, *break this spell* [*diesen Bann*] *in which it was confined.* (179; emphasis added)

I have been emphasizing all along that this ban or spell is itself the result of the interpellations, the various forms of symbolic investiture, that inscribe us in a symbolic space and tradition, endow us with the "dignities" of personhood.[58] Rosenzweig's paradoxical claim is that the shame that emerges under the impact of the "shock" of love—which is, after all, another sort of interpellation or summons—is in some sense a shame with regard to these very dignities, their tendency to assume the quality of defense mechanisms. Against

---

57. Given the connection Rosenzweig emphasizes between the metaethical self and the understanding of *tragedy* elaborated in Attic Greece, we might say that the superego sponsors a disavowal of the tragic aspect of human existence. It was precisely such a disavowal that Nietzsche so powerfully criticized in *The Birth of Tragedy*.

58. I refer, once more, to Agamben's remarks concerning the notion of *dignitas*. See *Remnants of Auschwitz*, 66.

what? Against the kernel of "indignity"—or, to borrow Schreber's term, of *Ludertum*—produced *by* every symbolic investiture. In some sense, then, love makes it possible to suspend, if only momentarily, our defenses with respect to this unnerving by-product of the processes and procedures of our socio-symbolic authorization. At such moments, the persuasive consistency of positive Being, the world of social relations (and its distribution of dignity), shines forth in the illumination of its contingency.

For Levinas, whose thought is deeply informed by Rosen-zweig's work, shame marks a break with the posture of the knowing, sovereign subject:

> The event of putting into question is the shame of the I for its
> naïve spontaneity, for its sovereign coincidence with itself in
> the identification of the Same. This shame is a movement in a
> direction opposed to that of consciousness, which returns tri-
> umphantly to itself and rests upon itself. To feel shame is to ex-
> pel oneself from this rest. . . . [59]

In the pages that follow I will be concerned with the difference between such an "expulsion" from rest—which we can think of as an awakening to, as an *aliveness to otherness*—and the "insomnia" proper to the superego.

---

59.   Levinas, *Basic Philosophical Writings*, 17.

CHAPTER FOUR

Responsibility beyond the Superego

I

Following Schelling's lead, Rosenzweig links the paradoxical materiality of the Other—his or her non-thing-like Thingness—to the enigma of human freedom. That is, when we encounter the Other in his or her singularity, we encounter that which in the Other *contracts from* all predicative being (and the matrix of relations established through it) in the very act of *contracting* predicates. When we encounter the Other in his or her answerability for his or her predicates (as the basis of any answerability to another human being), we encounter not an additional predicate but rather *the characteristic way the Other "contracts" his or her predicates.* It is this characteristic mode of "contraction" that for Rosenzweig most powerfully testifies to the fact of human freedom, to that in a human being which can most truly say "I." What, in other words, makes me me, what accounts for the force of the sentence "I am, no matter what, still me," is human freedom.[1]

---

1. For Schelling, freedom is most profoundly at work in the act by which a person "chooses" their character. In the second draft of

Rosenzweig's wager in the *Star of Redemption* is that this capacity to say "I" only becomes manifest, only truly becomes a part of life, in and through the response to the passionate call of one's proper name. Without this call and response, freedom remains in some sense impacted, "protocosmic," under the dominance of the force of "contraction" in the sense of a withdrawal and refusal that can, as I have been arguing, nonetheless serve as a support of our psychic attachment to existing social reality. With the call and response and its distinctive mode of temporalization, however, this complex accommodation to the matrix of social-symbolic relations and identifications in and through which we otherwise find our place in the world, is, for the eternity of a moment, suspended (this call and response is, in a word, where and how *eternity enters time*). To respond to love's interpellation—to its passionate utterances—is, I want to suggest, to momentarily suspend the force of the interpellations—the performative utterances—that otherwise invest us with socially intelligible identities, locate us within an established set of social relations of production and exchange.[2] Indeed, Rosenzweig explicitly reserves the term *relation* or *relationship* [*Beziehung*] for the socio-symbolic systems to which we surrender ourselves in our predicative being, on the basis of our *talents* (recall Rosenzweig's letter to Friedrich Meinecke). As he puts it in the "Germ Cell,"

> All relationships [*Beziehungen*] take place only between third persons; the system is the world in the form of the third person; and not merely the theoretical system, but just as man himself becomes an object, as soon as he wants *to make* some-

---

the *Weltalter*, Schelling emphasizes the persistence of this "deed": "The primordial deed which makes a man genuinely himself precedes all individual actions; but immediately after it is put into exuberant freedom, this deed sinks into the night of unconsciousness. This is not a deed that could happen once and then stop; it is a permanent deed, a never-ending deed, and consequently it can never again be brought before consciousness." *Abyss of Freedom/Ages of the World*, trans. Judith Norman (Ann Arbor: University of Michigan Press, 1997), 181.

2. In an essay on Schelling's *Weltalter* fragments, Jürgen Habermas notes that for Schelling, "[c]ontraction is made of harder stuff than negation, is, as it were, endowed with a surplus of moral energy surpassing the logical category." Love, for both Schelling and Rosenzweig, is a specific way of letting this moral energy become effective in the world. See Jürgen Habermas, *Theorie und Praxis. Sozialphilosophische Studien* (Frankfurt am Main: Suhrkamp, 1993), 195.

thing with or of himself, *he steps into the third person*, he stops being I (first and last name), he becomes the "human being" (with his palm branch).[3]

Rosenzweig's "psychotheological" point is that insofar as love itself—including, above all, love of God—is conceived on the model of a *relation*, a giving of oneself to a relation [*Hingabe*], God, too, remains within the register of the third person. This, then, is the crux of Rosenzweig's critique of pantheism:

> For the human being as *B* in this theoretical-practical system of third persons even God is only in the third person, only *A*. . . . Spinoza writes of this human being—and Goethe subscribes to it—that he who loves God may not demand that God love him in return. After all, how could he?! In the purity of his bosom there surges an aspiration to give himself voluntarily to a Higher Purer Unknown One out of gratitude—it is love in the third person, the He gives himself up to the It, no You becomes audible, and thus there one cannot speak of an I, and only the I can "demand" love. . . . All love here is surrender [*Hingabe*], a surrender whose simile can be *any* surrender of any kind. . . . ("Germ Cell," 53–54)

To return to the context of intersubjectivity, the contrast Rosenzweig proposes is, thus, ultimately one between *relation* and *encounter*: between love in the third person, love on the basis of our predicative being—our knowable "whatness" or "essence"—and revelatory love,

---

3. Franz Rosenzweig, "'Germ Cell' of the *Star of Redemption*," in *Franz Rosenzweig's "The New Thinking,"* ed. and trans. Barbara E. Galli and Alan Udoff (Syracuse: Syracuse University Press, 1999), 53. Subsequent references are given in the text. In Emmanuel Levinas's terms, the human being with his palm branch is the Other who has become faceless: "But when I have grasped the other (*autrui*) in the opening of being in general, as an element of the world where I stand, where I have seen him *on the horizon*, I have not looked at him in the face, I have not encountered his face." See Emmanuel Levinas, *Basic Philosophical Writings*, ed. Adriaan Peperzak, Simon Critchley, and Robert Bernasconi (Bloomington: Indiana University Press, 1996), 9. In my understanding, this face is always "distorted," always marred by a pathological tic, a trace of *jouissance*.

love as eventful encounter with the Other in his or her death-driven singularity, the uncanny locus of human freedom:

> "Essence" is the concept under which the world of objects, the world of $A = B$, arranges itself—essence, the universal [*das Allgemeine*], which gathers all singulars [*alles Einzelne*] under it, because it "precedes" all that is singular. Because it knows that human beings in general, "all" human beings, or the world in general, all things, are brothers to each other, *for this reason* the Stoic "loves," the Spinozist "loves" his neighbor. Against such love that arises out of the essence, the universal [*dem Allgemeinen*], stands the other that rises out of the event, that is out of the most particular (thing) there is [*dem Allerbesondersten was es gibt*]. This particular goes step by step from one particular to the next particular, from one neighbor to the next neighbor, and denies love to the furthest until it can be love of neighbor. The concept of order of this world is thus not the universal [*das Allgemeine*], neither the *arche* nor the *telos*, neither the natural nor the historical unity, but rather the singular, the event, *not beginning or end, but center of the world*. ("Germ Cell," 56–57)

Again, the crucial point here is that revelatory love is addressed not, as Rosenzweig writes, to my "brother in forest and grove, in rock and water," but rather to *what is most characteristic of the Other:* the always contingent, singular, and, in some sense, "demonic" way in which he or she contracts a foothold in Being. If revelation is, as Rosenzweig puts it, "capable of being a *center* point, a fixed, immovable centerpoint," it is only because

> it happens to the *point*, to the motionless, deaf, immovable point, the defiant I, the "I am when all is said and done." My "freedom," and to be sure not my freedom as the philosophers lie about it, in that they draw off from it the red blood of arbitrariness and let it run into the vessel of "sensuousness," of "drive," of "motives," and admit as freedom only the bloodless residue of obedience to the law. Rather the total freedom, my full, dull, irresponsible arbitrariness, my whole "this is how I

am when all is said and done," without which every freedom
of philosophers is lame from birth. ("Germ Cell," 57–58)

The paradox of revelatory love—as opposed to what we can
refer to as *relational surrender*—is, thus, that it in some sense reveals
nothing. It is a love in whose light no new predicate, no new content,
becomes manifest beyond the "nothing"—in Schelling's terms, the
nonbeing—of the demonic, tautological self-sameness testifying to
our freedom. Rosenzweig's argument is, in essence, that the *anam-
nesis* of this freedom, vividly conceptualized above all by Kant and
Schelling as that which cannot be captured in "relationships," can
become the basis of a specifically *modern* and philosophically rigorous renewal of the concept and experience of revelation.[4] My opening to the Other in his or her metaethical selfhood, my urgent sense
of answerability to this "nothing" of death-driven singularity in all
its insistent and idiosyncratic expressivity, is, for Rosenzweig, coterminous with the call of divine love. When we experience this urgency—when we are, as it were, seized by our "Neighbor-Thing"—
we are at that moment in the midst of something that both subtends
and exceeds the twoness of the encounter. Put somewhat differently:
the shift within a twoness from the part–whole logic of socio-
symbolic *relations* to the part–part logic of ethical *encounter*—these
are parts which are not parts of any whole—this very shift *is*, for
Rosenzweig, where and how human beings register the impact of
divine love.[5]

4. In the *Star*, Rosenzweig criticizes most post-Kantian thought for its domestication of the Kantian discovery. This domestication takes the form of assimilating the
fact of human freedom to an aspect of positive Being, of transposing freedom qua "miracle *in* the phenomenal world [*Wunder in der Erscheinungswelt*]" into freedom qua "miracle *of* the phenomenal world [*Wunder der Erscheinungswelt*]." *The Star of Redemption*,
trans. William W. Hallo (Notre Dame: University of Notre Dame Press, 1985), 10.

5. In response to questions concerning this very link between ethics and divinity, Levinas put it this way: "Is morality possible without God? I answer with a question: is divinity possible without relation to a human Other? Is such a thing possible in
Judaism? Consider Jeremiah, Chapter 22, or Isaiah 58:7: 'to bring to your house the
poor who are outcast.' The direct encounter with God, *this* is a Christian concept. As
Jews, we are always a threesome: I and you and the Third who is in our midst. And
only as a Third does He reveal Himself." Emmanuel Levinas, "Ideology and Idealism,"
trans. Sandford Ames and Arthur Lesley, in *The Levinas Reader*, ed. Sean Hand (Cambridge: Basil Blackwell, 1989), 247. And in another formulation: "The idea of the infinite . . . conserves for reflection the paradoxical knot which is already tied to religious

What transpires, then, in the opening of $B = B$—the formula of the metaethical self—to another $B = B$, is indeed a *tran-spirare:* the passage of divine breath—its "Adam, where are *you?*"—whereby the self can become a soul, gain a foothold not merely in Being but in what the Judeo-Christian tradition refers to as the Kingdom, the "world to come." This is, however, not some other place or time, some other order or totality of beings, but rather *a specific way of opening to the Other* in the place and time we already inhabit; it is, in a word, a specific way—and, at least potentially, an everyday way—of being in *the midst of life*, being open toward the passionate and often enigmatic insistence of what is singular about the Other. Rosenzweig's crucial insight is that this capacity for ethical encounter cannot be understood as some sort of spontaneous developmental achievement, as the simple and, as it were, organic unfolding of an essential human endowment, but rather as an *event* belonging to what I have referred to as the "psychotheology of everyday life." To borrow a phrase from Stanley Cavell, what Rosenzweig proposes might be characterized as a "philosophy of the (*eventual*) everyday":[6]

> All *B*s are made brothers, for all are interchangeable with each other, every *B* can become the *A* to the other. Not even once does the thought-bridge lead from $B = B$ to other $B = B$s: the bridge, the = sign, is constructed in the $B = B$ itself, it does not lead out of it. Only that from One $A = A$ the Word went out to $B = B$, only this leads $B = B$ out beyond itself, and only in this *event* that happened to it can it think another $B = B$, to which the same thing happened, a neighbor, who is like You. Not out of his own essence and out of the purity of his own heart does he discover the other, but out of the *happening* which happened to him and the deafness of his heart. ("Germ Cell," 56)

---

revelation. Revelation, which is from the start linked in its *concreteness* to obligations toward humans—the idea of God as love of the neighbor—is 'knowledge' of a God who, offering himself in this 'opening,' would also remain absolutely other or transcendent." Levinas, *Basic Philosophical Writings*, 155–56.

6. Stanley Cavell, *This New yet Unapproachable America. Lectures after Emerson after Wittgenstein* (Albuquerque: Living Batch Press, 1989), 46; emphasis added.

Rosenzweig's claim is, we might say, that without the language game of religion—of God—we lose the relevant possibilities of life with the *meta*ethical self, that uncanny gap/protrusion that troubles every "technique" of the self.[7] If the ethical "regulation" of one's relation to oneself and to others is to include the metaethical dimension, then one cannot, Rosenzweig argues, dispense with this language game.

It was precisely his conception of the midst of life as including, as being fundamentally oriented by, the metaethical dimension of the Other, that also led Rosenzweig to his critique of Goethe, whose life and work have, of course, been traditionally understood as offering the exemplary modern embodiment of an affirmation of dwelling in the midst or middle of life. As Rosenzweig himself emphasizes, Goethe too, with his purely creaturely prayer, his "prayer to his own fate," was "entirely at home in the world" (283); he fully overcomes, so to speak, the attitude of the child in Robert Walser's story "The End of the World," who, as we saw in chapter 1, flees from the middle of life and rushes, with apocalyptic fervor, toward the "end of the world." Childlikeness, for Goethe, stands rather for the capacity to be fully in the moment, to accept each instant as a grace granted to us. In his discussion of the Stoic and Epicurean dimensions of this Goethean "wisdom of the child," Pierre Hadot has noted that it affirms "in the first place, that one instant of happiness is equivalent to an eternity; and secondly, that one instant of existence contains the whole eternity of the cosmos. In Goethean terms," Hadot concludes, "this . . . idea could be expressed by saying that the instant is the symbol of eternity."[8] Rosenzweig's strategy in

---

7. I think that Cavell ultimately has the same point in mind—and would thus count, for Rosenzweig, as a "new thinker"—when he writes, apropos of the distinction between *knowing* another mind—the reef on which all skepticism founders—and *acknowledging* another mind: "The withdrawals and approaches of God can be looked upon as tracing the history of our attempts to overtake and absorb acknowledgment by knowledge; God would be the name of that impossibility." Stanley Cavell, *Must We Mean What We Say? A Book of Essays* (Cambridge: Cambridge University Press, 1995), 347. Cavell has elsewhere also emphasized the uncanniness of the Other's claim on our acknowledgment; what I have referred to as ethical encounter thus involves a situation in which it makes sense to say that "the familiar [is] invaded by another familiar." Cavell, *Unapproachable America*, 47.

8. Pierre Hadot, *Philosophy as a Way of Life. Spiritual Exercises from Socrates to Foucault*, ed. Arnold Davidson, trans. Michael Chase (Oxford: Blackwell, 1995), 233.

the *Star* is, in a certain sense, to show that this aesthetics of the symbol, above all when applied to life qua "work of art," still functions as a form of defense with respect to the anxiety occasioned by the Other, by the *traumatic* dimension of the encounter with what is in our midst. And for Rosenzweig, eternity enters time precisely through such an encounter.[9]

II

"Every *B* can become the *A* to the other"—with this formulation, Rosenzweig is perhaps alluding to Marx's elaboration of the commodity form (which was, in turn, prefigured in Schelling's generative theory of predication and Hegel's theory of judgment). For Marx, one will recall, the entire problem of value begins with a contingent equation or identification: one commodity is posited as being of equal value to another commodity. And as Marx notes, the "whole mystery of the form of value lies hidden in this simple form," in this initial "contraction" of value.[10] In this first and contingent relation between two use-values, the value of the first commodity, which Marx calls the *relative* form of value, is expressed in the use-value of the second, which he refers to as the *equivalent* form of value. To cite

---

Hadot cites Goethe's late poem, "Elegy," to illustrate this posture:

> Do like me, then: with joyful wisdom
> Look the instant in the eye! Do not delay!
> Hurry! Run to greet it, lively and benevolent,
> Be it for action, for joy or for love!
> Wherever you may be, be like a child, wholly and always;
> Then you will be the All; and invincible.

9.   As Rosenzweig writes in the *Star*, "The life of Goethe, this most blissful of human lives, was the brief inimitable moment where it really might have seemed as if creaturely prayer could be prayed all by itself. Seen from this moment, time really appears to stand still. . . . But temporality is not eternity. Goethe was the most alive of men, but even his life was only temporally [*zeitlich*] alive. . . . That which is temporal requires the eternal for support" (288). We should also note that "Elegy" itself underlines the difficulties of sustaining the aesthetic wisdom/ideology to which it nonetheless seems dedicated. Rosenzweig's critique of the Goethean aesthetics of the symbol is more systematically elaborated by Walter Benjamin in his *The Origin of German Tragic Drama*, trans. John Osborne (London: NLB, 1977), where he actually makes use of Rosenzweig's understanding of tragedy and the metaethical self.

10.   Karl Marx, *Capital*, vol. 1, trans. Ben Fowkes (New York: Vintage, 1977), 139. Subsequent references are given in the text.

Marx's first example of the different roles played in this bit of economic alchemy, whereby a *contingent* use-value is transformed into the "sublime objectivity" (144) of Value, we can imagine that twenty yards of linen is exchanged for, and thus posited as being equivalent to, one coat (in the idiom of mathematics: "Let one coat equal twenty yards of linen"): "The linen expresses its value in the coat; the coat serves as the material in which that value is expressed. The first commodity plays an active role, the second a passive one" (139). And as Marx further notes, the "relative form of value and the equivalent form are two inseparable moments, which belong to and mutually condition each other; but, at the same time, they are mutually exclusive or opposed extremes, i.e. poles of the expression of value" (139–40). Marx underlines the greater syntactic generality of his discussion of commodities by noting that

> in a certain sense, a man is in the same situation as a commodity. As he neither enters into the world in possession of a mirror, nor as a Fichtean philosopher who can say "I am I," a man first sees and recognizes himself in another man. Peter only relates to himself as a man through his relation to another man, Paul, in whom he recognizes his likeness. With this, however, Paul also becomes from head to toe, in his physical form as Paul, the form of appearance of the species man for Peter. (144)

Marx's elaboration of the various phases of the form of value, from the elementary or accidental to the total or expanded form, to the general form, and, finally, to the money form, can be understood as a general syntactic theory of what Rosenzweig refers to as the *system of life in the third person.*[11]

As Marx continues his elaboration of this "system," "the simple form of value automatically passes over into a more complete form" (154). That is, the value of commodity *A*—the linen, in Marx's example—can express its value not only in commodity *B*—a coat—but in any number of other commodities against which it can be

---

11.   The most detailed and forceful presentation of this syntactic generality can be found in Jean-Joseph Goux, *Symbolic Economies. After Marx and Freud*, trans. Jennifer Curtiss Gage (Ithaca: Cornell University Press, 1990).

exchanged (*B*, *C*, *D*, . . .). "The isolated expression of *A*'s value is thus transformed into the indefinitely expandable series of different simple expressions of that value" (154). It is really only at this stage that we enter a dimension of generality, or as Marx puts it, "that this value first shows itself as being, in reality, a congealed quantity of undifferentiated human labor" (155). This apparently universal dimension is, however, still hindered, constrained by contradiction. For not only does the series of representations of value extend indefinitely for any single commodity occupying the place of relative value, "each equivalent commodity is itself involved in other relationships, where it in turn acts as relative form to an infinite series of equivalents. . . . It is a situation of rivalry, of crisis, of conflict. A commodity cannot express its own value once and for all, cannot fix its own price in an absolute universal estimate. It is caught in the interminable contradictions of a *relativism* in which no one component prevails. . . . "[12]

The solution to this crisis in which every single commodity is linked to an endless series of other commodities that represent its value for it is achieved only when every commodity yields its right, so to speak, to represent value for the others to one single, exceptional commodity, which is set apart and thereby assumes a different level of "being," becomes, to use Schelling's locution, *das Aussprechende*, the sole speaker of value, for *all the others*.[13] This exceptional commodity Marx calls the *universal* or *general equivalent*:

> This new form . . . expresses the values of the world of commodities through one single kind of commodity set apart from the rest, through the linen for example, and thus represents the value of all commodities by means of their equality with linen. Through its equation with linen, the value of every commodity is now not only differentiated from its own use-value, but from all use-values, and is, by that very fact, expressed as that which is common to all commodities. (158)

In this form of value, a "single commodity . . . therefore has the form of direct exchangeability with all other commodities, in other words

---

12. Ibid., 15.
13. Schelling uses this term in the various drafts of the *Weltalter*.

it has a directly social form because, and in so far as, no other commodity is in this situation" (161). As Jean-Joseph Goux suggests, it is as if commodity exchange had now emphatically entered into the realm of *logos:* this "is an elegant solution; it is *reason* itself—not simply because it then becomes possible to settle on a reasonable price, a 'square deal' . . . but also . . . because it introduces measure into the community. Now values . . . recognize each other (in the same ideal)."[14]

The fourth and final phase of this genesis is the so-called money form in which the general equivalent attains "objective fixedness and general social validity." As Marx continues, the "specific kind of commodity with whose natural form the equivalent form is socially interwoven now becomes the money commodity, or serves as money. It becomes its specific social function, and consequently its social monopoly, to play the part of universal equivalent within the world of commodities." And as Marx finally notes, "the universal equivalent form . . . has . . . by social custom . . . become entwined with the specific natural form of the commodity gold" (162).[15]

The reason for this brief excursus on the commodity form is to emphasize that for both Marx and Rosenzweig the point is not the smooth running of the symbolic system of substitutions and valuations but rather that relations of exchange—and that means all socio-symbolic systems through which what is individual acquires a general and generic value/identity—always leave a remainder, an insistent and troubling surplus for which no equivalent value can be posited. And for both thinkers, this troubling surplus that for the

---

14. Goux, *Symbolic Economies,* 16.

15. As many commentators have noted, the function of the general equivalent in the realm of commodities is syntactically homologous to that of the sovereign in the realm of "subjects." Slavoj Žižek has elucidated Lacan's understanding of the so-called master or sovereign signifier (in Lacan's notation, S_1) by correlating three otherwise inconsistent versions of Lacan's formulations on the "subject of the signifier" with the stages of Marx's genesis of the general equivalent: "1. The simple form; 'for *a* signifier, *another* signifier represents the subject' (i.e. '*a* signifier represents the subject for *another* signifier'); 2. The expanded form: 'for *a* signifier, *any* of the other signifiers can represent the subject'; 3. The general form: '*a* (one) signifier represents the subject for *all the other* signifiers.'" See Slavoj Žižek, *For They Know Not What They Do. Enjoyment as a Political Factor* (London: Verso, 1991), 24.

most part functions as the driving force of the symbolic system can become the locus of a break with it, a site where the possibility of unplugging from the dominance of the sovereign/general equivalent can open. Indeed, that opening *is* what Rosenzweig understands by revelation. Revelation is thus not so much the positing of an alternative and competing standard of value as an intervention into the very syntax by which values are determined and to which we are bound in our life with values. In far more mundane and psychological terms, I would say that Rosenzweig's conception of revelation concerns the event of changing direction in one's life, of opening to the possibility of fundamentally new possibilities beyond our "relational surrender," our domination by the currency and measure of our predicative being. Revelation is a paradoxical mode of opening to what seems most fatefully "demonic" about us, what "sticks out" from our predicative being; it is paradoxical because it involves both an affirmation and a negation of this demonic core.

III

As I have argued, this "demonic" core is occasioned or, to use Jean Laplanche's terms, "implanted" or "intromitted," by enigmatic messages emanating from the Other. As I also suggested, this Other can be understood not only as another subject but also as the symbolic tradition and order into which one is born, which in turn always includes traces of lost forms of life, "hieroglyphs in the desert." But it also includes, is traversed by, struggles and antagonisms that render this order *enigmatically inconsistent.* This inconsistency is something different from incompleteness, from a reference to a lack that could be filled by an element imported from the outside; inconsistency cannot, in other words, simply be equated with *scarcity* of some sort. In the case of a child, these enigmatic messages come, first and foremost, from adult caregivers. We gain a ground or foothold in the world of *Mitsein*, of being-together, to the extent that we struggle to translate these messages into possible questions. Our entire being is in some sense permeated by these unconscious efforts at making the enigmas by which we feel ourselves addressed—these scraps of *validity in excess of any meaning*—make sense (this is what it means to discharge an excitation). The very core of what we think of as our individuality, our characteristic way of assuming our place amid the socio-symbolic relations of exchange that constitute our shared world, can be understood as the *pulse* of these fantasmatic efforts. The deep sense of psychic rigidity or "stuckness" that is of interest to psychoanalysis is, we might say, nothing but a persistence of this pulse of *meaningless yet valid* behavior that constitutes our unconscious *attachment* to as well as *defense* against the Other's "exciting" secret or enigma.

The fundamental problem for both Freud and Rosenzweig is that of intervening into this rigidity, this pulse of undeadness, of releasing us from a repetition compulsion that permeates our being, that in some peculiar sense *is who we are*. That, I am suggesting, is what it means to change direction in one's life. It happens when we are able to find ourselves, if only momentarily, in what we might call the *void of our character*, its element of tautological self-reference, its $B = B$. As we have seen, Rosenzweig's project is largely dedicated to thinking through the event-structure of this happening, its difference from any sort of developmental achievement or unfolding of a pregiven essence, its status as a kind of *creatio ex nihilo*.

In his own speculations on these matters, Jonathan Lear has suggested that we think of such changes of direction as the very meaning of human happiness, of what it means, in psychoanalytic terms, to catch a "lucky break" in life. Such breaks, are, as Lear puts it, a sort of "existential sabbath," "an occasion for opening up new possibilities, possibilities not included in any established structures." Happiness, Lear suggests, arrives when it becomes possible to appropriate the "possibilities for new possibilities" which are, as he puts it, "breaking out all the time":

> But if psychoanalysis lies outside the ethical [that is: addresses the *meta*-ethical self; E.L.S.], how does it promote happiness? Here we need to go back to an older English usage of happiness in terms of happenstance: the experience of chance things working out well rather than badly. Happiness, on this interpretation, is not the ultimate goal of our teleologically organized strivings—but the ultimate ateleological moment: a chance event going well for us. Quite literally: a lucky break. Analysis puts us in a position to take advantage of certain

kinds of chance occurrences: those breaks in psychological structure which are caused by too much of too much. This isn't a teleological occurrence, but a taking-advantage of the disruption of previous attempts to construct a teleology. If one thinks about it . . . one will see that it is in such fleeting moments that we find real happiness.[16]

We would do well to understand such fleeting moments as exactly what is meant by, to use Harold Bloom's phrase once again, "the blessings of more life" in contrast to any sort of augmentation of our life amid relations of production and exchange. In Rosenzweig's terms, these are moments when the tautological nonsense that is our metaethical self becomes momentarily uncoupled from our life of relational surrender. At such moments, the enigma of our legitimation within the part–whole relations that constitute our symbolic universe converts, as it were, from being the *driving force* of these very efforts at surrender, or *Hingabe*, to being *just drive*. In the more familiar terms of Freud's structural theory of the mind, these are moments, I am suggesting, when the superego's impossible demands become manifest as bits of nonsense that permeate our being but cannot, not even in any form of recovered memory, be rendered as consistent, meaningful communications. At such moments of conversion or *Umkehr*, the very basis of our capture by existing social relations—our biopolitical animation or undeadness—becomes the locus of an opening "beyond" it.[17] The reason I use quota-

16.   Jonathan Lear, *Happiness, Death and the Remainder of Life* (Cambridge: Harvard University Press, 2000), 129. Happiness is, of course, etymologically related to happening. The idea that new possibilities are breaking out all the time is what Rosenzweig tries to capture with the concept of the "metalogical world." See especially the *Star*, 45.

17.   Žižek has provided two nice examples of such a conversion as it is staged in cinematic representations of totalitarian societies. Apropos of the music in the Terry Gilliam film, *Brazil*, Žižek writes that "throughout the film, it seems that the idiotic, intrusive rhythm of 'Brazil' serves as a support for totalitarian enjoyment, i.e., that it condenses the fantasy frame of the 'crazy' totalitarian social order that the film depicts. But at the very end, when his resistance is apparently broken by the savage torture to which he has been subjected, the hero escapes his torturers by beginning to whistle 'Brazil!' Although functioning as a support for the totalitarian order, fantasy is then at the same time the leftover of the real that enables us to 'pull ourselves out' . . . " Slavoj Žižek, *Looking Awry. An Introduction to Jacques Lacan through Popular Culture* (Cambridge: MIT Press, 1991), 128. The same dynamic operates in Rainer Werner Fass-

tion marks when I speak here of a "beyond" is because the conversion at stake pertains not to a passage to a realm beyond the world but rather to one beyond or across the fantasies that in some sense hinder our openness in and to the world, our being in the *midst of life*.

In a first approach, we might put this in terms of our conception of human loneliness. The protocosmos, as Rosenzweig understands it, entails a certain metaphysical picture of human loneliness, that is, loneliness understood as a form of a limiting and substantial *containment* that precludes encounter all the while inscribing us in part–whole relations; the conversion Rosenzweig has in mind is not to a state "beyond" all loneliness—that would be to remain within this metaphysical picture of limiting containers—but rather to a different conception and experience of human loneliness. For some form of loneliness—the loneliness of what I have referred to as death-driven singularity—necessarily persists as the basis of all authentic encounter (that is the meaning of Rosenzweig's characterization of the protocosmos as *immerwährend*, ever-enduring). There is a form of loneliness, in other words, that *is* openness to what is other, and revelation is the event of our conversion to it. It converts the protocosmos from being the hindrance to, from being a defense against, encounter to being its very basis or condition of possibility. As I put it earlier, the Kingdom, as I take Rosenzweig to understand it, is not about the reanimation of the dead—the passage to a realm beyond the one of our vulnerability and mortality—but concerns rather the deanimation of the undead (undeadness understood as the persistence of *metaphysical* loneliness). We enter the Kingdom not by transcending social relations but by intervening into and converting our mode of capture by social relations. The paradox Rosenzweig is getting at is that the very (unconscious) fantasies at work in this capture actually keep us at a kind of distance from life. Revelation is ultimately nothing but a clearing away of the fantasies that confine our energies within an ultimately *defensive* protocosmic exis-

---

binder's *Lili Marleen* in which the title song—the real protagonist of the film—is played in endless repetition until its sentimental charm becomes nearly unbearable. "Here, again," Žižek writes, "its status is unclear: totalitarian power (personified by Goebbels) tries to manipulate it, to use it to capture the imagination of the tired soldiers, but the song escapes its grasp like a genie released from a bottle. It begins to lead a life of its own—nobody can master its effects." Ibid., 128.

tence—our various forms of "Egyptomania"—that keep us at a distance from our answerability within everyday life and, to use Lear's formulation, from the possibilities for new possibilities that are all the time breaking out within it. Again, the paradox is this: a certain fantasmatic *distance* is correlative to our psychic *capture* by existing social relations—to what I have referred to as our "relational surrender"—and thus to the foreclosure of the possibility of new possibilities that can only truly arise in the eventful space of encounter.[18]

The paradox in question here is, as I have already indicated, the paradox of the *superego*. This psychic agency that sustains our attachment to the norms of a community functions not so much at the level of belief as in the form of a pressure or urgency that can, in turn, incite transgression of and, thus, apparent distance to, those very norms. When we transgress the rule of law of a community, that is often when we are most fully in the thrall of the superego's power. "What 'holds together' a community most deeply," as Žižek has put it, "is not so much identification with the Law that regulates the community's 'normal' everyday circuit, but rather *identification with a specific form of transgression of the Law, of the Law's suspension* (in psychoanalytic terms, with a specific form of *enjoyment*)."[19] Superego

18. Again, Rosenzweig emphasizes that the opening to the possibility for new possibilities that is constitutive of the (metalogical) world is not a developmental achievement but rather requires a performative supplement: "Life is assured of citizenship in the kingdom only by becoming immortal. In order to become manifest form, the world thus requires an effect from without in addition to its own inner growth, the growth of life which is precarious because never certain of enduring. This effect affects its vitality in the act of redemption." *Star, 225*. I understand this "immortality" as the "blessings of more life," that is, as the vitality correlative to the deanimation of undeadness.

19. Slavoj Žižek, *Metastases of Enjoyment. Six Essays on Woman and Causality* (London: Verso, 1994), 55. One of Žižek's examples for the workings of superego is the "solidarity-in-guilt" that was operative in communities in the American South before World War II, "where the reign of the official, public Law is accompanied by its shadowy double, the nightly terror of Ku Klux Klan, with its lynchings of powerless blacks: a (white) man is easily forgiven minor infractions of the Law, especially when they can be justified by a 'code of honour'; the community still recognizes him as 'one of us.' Yet he will be effectively excommunicated, perceived as 'not one of us,' the moment he disowns the specific form of *transgression* that pertains to this community— say, the moment he refuses to partake in the ritual lynchings by the Klan, or even reports them to the Law (which, of course, does not want to hear about them, since they exemplify its own hidden underside)." Ibid., 55.

is conceived here as the agency that demands this enjoyment, as the voice whose monotonous command is "Enjoy!" This is the paradox missed over and over again by the protagonists of Kafka's novels who are in each case, to use Gershom Scholem's formulation, confronted by an excess of validity over meaning that drives them into a desperate search for a meaning, a search that in some sense becomes identical with everyday life itself. The various forms of obscene, often sadomasochistic, sexual activity that transpire, for example, in the shadows of the courts in *The Trial* are, in the end, not so much spaces where the Law fails to reach but rather *the superegoic form of its reach*, the way in which a "too much," an excess of validity over meaning, achieves a certain degree of organization.

This is all, perhaps, another way of formulating Laplanche's fundamental thesis: every induction into the domain of socio-symbolic relations is also, at least to some extent, a *seduction;* one's solidarity with the spirit of one's family/community/institution is always in part sustained by the "spirit world" of transgressive enjoyment structured in fantasy. The crucial point here is that this fantasmatic transgression/transcendence of the governing rules of social relations is at least to some degree *immanent to their effectivity;* fantasy is, as it were, where we "get off" on the enigmatic inconsistency of those very relations. We might say, then, that "getting into" a form of life, entering the domain of its normativity or *Verbindlichkeit*, includes a dimension of "getting off." This is the libidinal/ibidinal dimension of the Pascalian wager at work in everyday life; in every form of life there is an element of subjection to—or better, *seduction by*—the uncomprehended letter that is not so much dead as undeadening.

This excitational residue of the various forms of symbolic investiture that—more or less successfully—install us in social reality is, as I've suggested, precisely what Freud saw when he noted, in his famous case study of obsessional neurosis, that the Ratman's face manifested a *"horror at pleasure of his own of which he himself was unaware."*[20] Freud touches upon the Kafkan dimension of this uncanny animation when he writes, "We are not used to feeling strong affects

---

20. Freud, *Notes upon a Case of Obsessional Neurosis*, in *The Standard Edition of the Complete Psychological Works*, ed. and trans. James Strachey (London: Hogarth Press, 1953–74), 10:166–67.

without their having any ideational content, and therefore, if the content is missing, we seize as a substitute upon another content which is in some way or other suitable, much as our police, when they cannot catch the right murderer, arrest a wrong one instead."[21] The paradox that Freud fails to notice, however—and here Kafka is the more radical social thinker than Freud—is that affect without ideational content, that is, the psychic registration of validity in excess of meaning, is *constitutive of the social bond itself.* The Ratman's obsessional disorder, which acquired much of its color and form through the story of the rat torture recounted by his captain during military exercises in Galicia, ought not to be separated from the former's mode of inscription in, his (ex)citation by, the institution in which he served with apparent distinction.[22] The gruesome details of the "oriental" torture became, I am suggesting, one of the "dialects" of the superego that sustained the Ratman's attachment to his social roles even as it unnerved and disoriented him.

Against the background of this superego dynamic whereby the peculiar doubling / intensification of public law by its obscene, superego underside is seen to bind the subject all the more effectively to existing social reality, revelation assumes a new countenance. Indeed, it has been my argument that Rosenzweig's work is largely an elaboration of this new face of revelation. According to this view, it does not so much provide the subject with a new law or cause with which to identify, some new set of precedents to repeat; rather, through the intervention of a different mode and trajectory of interpellation—again, one thinks of Rosenzweig's distinction between *Gebot* and *Gesetz*, commandment and law—it releases the subject

21. Ibid., 10:176.

22. The Ratman, who died as a prisoner of war in Russian captivity during World War I, had a generally good record as a soldier and reserve officer. According to his military dossier of 1900, he enjoyed a "quite serious, very diligent character, good intellectual gifts with like comprehension. Conforms to the requirements of his official position, and leads his section decisively and also independently both in fighting and in formation. . . . Reliable and smart behavior on the front, well instructed in the matters of weapons and firearms, can use his knowledge practically, shoots fairly well . . . eager and industrious . . . obedient and ready toward his superiors. Very friendly and companionable with his equals. And suitable by his good influence on subordinates." Quoted in Patrick J. Mahony, *Freud and the Ratman* (New Haven: Yale University Press, 1986), 8.

from what I have been characterizing as its "Egyptomania": its (for the most part unconscious) labors to translate superegoic pressure into a meaningful communication/legislation. It is a release, then, not so much from the call or *citation* by the law as from the *ex-citations induced by its superego supplement*. For Rosenzweig, the time and space of this release *is* the time and space of ethical encounter, a space where new possibilities of being-together, of responsiveness to the Other, can arise.

IV

These reflections allow us to articulate one of Rosenzweig's crucial and, no doubt, surprising contributions to the psychoanalytic understanding of monotheism in general and of Judaism in particular. Rather than being the ultimate religion of the superego as Freud argues in *Moses and Monotheism*, it turns out to be, if we take Rosenzweig's analysis of revelation seriously, just the opposite: Judaism, this first religion of revelation, can rather be understood as a kind of therapy directed precisely against the fantasmatic pressures of the superego and its tendency to keep the subject at a distance from his or her answerability within the world. That the superego can hinder a sense of answerability may sound paradoxical since the conventional Freudian understanding is that one only truly becomes answerable under the pressure of the superego. The gist of Rosenzweig's argument is, however, that answerability under such pressure is at best answerability in the *third person*—as a he, she, or it—rather than in the *first person*, as an *I* (and with respect to a *Thou*). This is the difference, as Jonathan Lear has suggested, between *accepting* responsibility and *holding* oneself responsible. "It seems," Lear writes, "that the cost of failing to *accept* responsibility for my drives, and thus incorporate them into the I, is that I become liable to *hold* myself responsible for them in a pathological way."[23]

Superego is the psychic agency that *polices one's identity*, one's place within the third-personal, part–whole relations that make up

---

23. Jonathan Lear, *Love and Its Place in Nature. A Philosophical Interpretation of Freudian Psychoanalysis* (New York: Farrar, Straus & Giroux, 1990), 174.

the cultural systems we inhabit, whereas revelation pertains to the possibility of an opening and a belonging-together on the basis of a nonrelational surplus in myself and in my neighbor. Superego discourse is, I am suggesting, a species of juridical—or rather, metajuridical—discourse; it is ultimately about law and the subject's always "exciting" inscription in law. Revelation, on the other hand, is an opening of a space of human possibilities organized around the claims made upon me by the Other insofar as he or she is singularly out-of-joint with respect to the social intelligibility produced by this inscription in law. The Other who invades my life with his or her passionate claims on my attention, desire, and care is, in other words, an Other filled with too much pressure, a surplus of excitations that have, to some extent, always already been organized as impossible, superegoic demands.

Here it might be worthwhile to recall briefly Freud's argument in *Moses and Monotheism*. According to Freud, the Jews in the course of their history have been able to reach the ethical and intellectual heights they have attained only because of a neurotic compulsion—a form of "stuckness"—at the core of their spiritual life. In his view, this compulsion bears witness to an immemorial guilt transmitted from generation to generation not simply by way of consciously elaborated traditions but also by way of some form of unconscious transmission that Freud tended to characterize in Lamarckian terms. As Freud would have it, this guilt is none other than the guilt incurred through the murder of Moses by the ancient Hebrews who could not sustain the social, cultural, and above all psychic losses that went hand in hand with the rigors of the monotheistic cult imposed on them by this strange Egyptian priest (Freud, of course, thought Moses to be a member of Akhenaten's inner circle who, after the rapid demise of the latter's monotheistic innovation, passed it on to the Hebrews). The losses correlative to the advent of monotheism—whether one agrees with Freud's story of Jewish ethnogenesis or not—can be understood as a series of traumatic cuts or separations: of the deity from plastic representation; of spirituality from magic, animism, and sexual ecstasy; of thinking from the fantasy of the omnipotence of thoughts; of death from the cult of the afterlife (call it separating from "Mummy" and all forms of "mummification"). Freud understood the contingent and historical condition of *diaspora* as simply the next link in this logical sequence: the separation of a people from a territory imagined to be proper to them.

For Freud, the murder of Moses, which metaphorically repeats the murder of the primal father that first released humankind from life in the horde and inaugurated the rule of reciprocity, was what ultimately guaranteed the survival of the Jews as a people and tradition. One of the fundamental laws of psychic life as Freud understood it was that fathers rule not as real individuals but rather as symbolic agencies represented by their *name*. The name of the father is, furthermore, always the name of the *dead* father, the father who has been aggressively set apart, expelled into the symbolic efficacy or transcendence correlative to his role as general equivalent of subjects within the kinship group or family collective. The social bond contracted under the auspices of the paternal law is, in a word, sustained by some form of murderous betrayal; *Moses and Monotheism* attempts to locate and elaborate the structural necessity of that betrayal within the Jewish tradition. But this, of course, is all another way of saying that the paternal law—in this case the law given by Moses—is sustained by a dynamic of transgression and culpabilization, that is, by superego. Our very obedience to the law testifies to the betrayal that sustains its efficacy. In the Freudian view, we are "in" a form of life, truly animated by its spirit, not so much when we agree with its basic rules, values, codes of conduct—its publicly affirmed conception of the "good"—but rather when we are *haunted by its spirits*, so to speak, plagued at some level of our being by the immemorial transgression *structurally transmitted* by the form of life itself and the narratives, rituals, myths that lend it its symbolic consistency.

This superego dynamic is preserved even if we displace the locus of transgression as Robert Paul has done in his brilliant reinterpretation of Freud's essay.[24] In contrast to Freud, Paul locates the problem of guilt not in the history or even prehistory of the Jews but rather within the structure of the foundational *myths* of the Judeo-Christian cultural system, myths that help to organize, in a determi-

---

24.   Robert Paul, *Moses and Civilization: The Meaning behind Freud's Myth* (New Haven: Yale University Press, 1996). Subsequent references are given in the text.

nate way, fundamental human anxieties, conflicts, and wishes arising within the ambivalent dynamic of generational succession. Paul borrows Richard Dawkins's notion of *memes*, the equivalent in a symbolic system of genetic codes in cellular life, to characterize the way in which these myths serve to reproduce a given cultural system. Noting that both memes and genes belong to a wider class of "replicators," meaning "anything in the universe of which copies are made," Paul suggests that

> a "memic" or cultural replicator accomplishes its work by channeling the motivation and capacities of human actors into activities that result in the reproduction of copies of the meme. . . . People who have been significantly informed by the same memic instructions can be said to be like each other and, indeed, to be related in a way directly analogous to the way people are genetically related: that is, by being realizations of, and providers of future copies of, the same instructions. (186)

This is a version of the notion I invoked earlier when I recast Freud's structural model of the psyche as the "Ego and the Ibid." The *libidinal* component of one's symbolic identity must be thought of as being "ibidinal," too: a largely unconscious *citation* of the authority guaranteeing one's rightful enjoyment of the predicates proper to it. Paul notes that the Torah as a whole is well suited to function as a source or generator of "ibidinal cathexis." "It is," he writes, "a symbol whose meaning, and ability to instruct authoritatively, comes from its own status as a self-created, self-referential symbol, or meme, and thus as a fixed point in relation to which all other symbols derive meaning, that derives its own meaning from nothing except itself" (187).

Paul's fundamental point is that the Mosaic "memes" actually do produce in their "offspring" a sense of guilt apropos of patricidal violence; the father in question, however, is not Moses but rather *Pharaoh*. As Paul summarizes this fundamental revision of Freud's argument,

> [the] destruction of Egypt is . . . a crime on Moses's hands. . . .
> Moses's rebellion is at once a patricide, since Pharaoh is Mo-

> ses's father; a deicide, since Pharaoh is a living god; a regicide,
> since Pharaoh is the ruler of the Egyptian empire; and a revolt
> of the servant against the master, since Moses leads the en-
> slaved Israelites against their overlord and taskmaster. . . . Be-
> cause of the guilt engendered by this deed the covenant on
> Mount Sinai is instituted, and from that guilt the Law gains
> its compulsory force. According to the Mosaic Law—which
> is, however, a statement of the more general human social
> principle of reciprocity—justice demands like for like: punish-
> ment, in talionic fashion, must match the crime. . . . Because
> this debt remains uncollected, the Israelites are violators of the
> Law *by virtue of the very events that led to its promulgation.* The
> Law itself, no matter how restrictive it may seem, protectively
> wards off the as-yet unexecuted and dreaded talionic punish-
> ment for the original crime. (210; emphasis added)

In this view, Moses introduces into the Jewish tradition a superego dynamic we might call *last cannibal syndrome*, borrowing from the witticism "There are no more cannibals; I ate the last one." Moses is such a "last cannibal" in that the deeds he performs in God's name leading to the revelation at Sinai are transgressions in the context of that same revelation. Moses thus does indeed have to "disappear," not, however, because he stands in for the primal father who must be *aufgehoben* into the rule of his name but rather because he was the agent or operator of the deeds that separated the Jews from their pagan surround; these deeds become, in light of the revelation at Sinai, crimes calling for atonement. The children of this revelation inherit not, as Freud thought, the crime committed against the culture hero but rather the founding crime of the culture hero himself. For both Freud and Paul, the compulsive nature of Jewish ethical strivings functions as *a mode of verification* of this very inheritance, a testimony to its "historical truth" (as Freud put it, in contrast to the "real" or "material" truth of historical events).[25]

---

25.   According to the logic of this account, Christ assumes the status of "last meal" that in principle ought to allow the offspring of the Judaic revelation—in es-sence, anyone who adopts/lets himself be "adopted" by the memic system of the Old Testament—to be finally cured of "last cannibal syndrome."

V

How are we to adjudicate these seemingly contradictory claims about the status of the superego in the ethical monotheism of the Jewish cultural system? We might begin by considering the critique of Freud's view offered by Yosef Yerushalmi in what is no doubt one of the most compelling engagements with *Moses and Monotheism* in the literature on Freud.[26] In the final part of his book, staged as a sort of monologue addressed to Freud's ghost, Yerushalmi suggests that Freud's sense of the inevitability of this superego dynamic, which in individual life is expressed in the Oedipus complex, is where Freud manifests his most distinctly "un-Jewish" attitude. Characterizing Freud's view as a "haunting vision of Eternal Return," Yerushalmi suggests that it lacks the "anticipation of a specific hope for the future," a hope announced, for example, in the prophet Malachi's verse on the reconciliation of the hearts of the fathers with the sons and the hearts of the sons with the fathers (3:24). As Yerushalmi finally puts it in his address to Freud, "it is on this question of hope or hopelessness, even more than on God or godlessness, that your teaching may be at its most un-Jewish."[27] More important for our purposes here, Yerushalmi further suggests that the hopefulness at issue in Judaism—its hope that is, for the "blessings of more life" rather than those that derive from the "foundation and augmentation of institutions"—need not imply the vision of a life *beyond the law* but can include, indeed be structured around, "the rigorous imperatives of the Law."[28] If the release from the punishing pressures of the superego is a form of grace, then it is, Yerushalmi argues, a grace *internal* to those rigorous imperatives, those elaborations of individual and collective obligations, rather than one that suspends the law in its "fulfillment." Again, this is precisely what Rosenzweig had argued apropos of the distinction between commandment and law, a distinction that no doubt helped make it possible for Rosenzweig to abandon his plans to convert to Christianity.

26.   Yosef Hayim Yerushalmi, *Freud's Moses. Judaism Terminable and Interminable* (New Haven: Yale University Press, 1991).

27.   Ibid., 95.

28.   Ibid., 94.

To return to Rosenzweig, we might begin by noting that in his own discussion of Judaism in the *Star* he places perhaps even greater emphasis than Freud on the dimension of loss, separation, and deterritorialization as constitutive of the Jewish people and tradition. In the *Star*, Rosenzweig in effect argues that a number of the anti-Semitic claims circulating in late-nineteenth- and early-twentieth-century European society pertaining to Jewish life and character, claims made famous, in part, by Richard Wagner in his notorious treatise, *Judaism in Music*, [29] were at some level correct. Jews, Rosenzweig asserts, do lack the passionate attachment to the things that constitute the primary libidinal "objects" of other historical peoples and nations, attachments that ultimately constitute their vitality and endurance as peoples and nations: land, territory, and architecture; regional and national languages; laws, customs, and institutions founded and augmented in the course of a people's history. In Rosenzweig's view, Jewish difference is fundamentally a difference in the structure of desire, in the relation to the void around which desire orbits. That the objects of Jewish desire—the land of its longing, for example—are deemed "holy," means that desire is *infinitized:* "This holiness increases the longing for what is lost, to infinity, and so the people can never be entirely at home in any other land" (300).[30] For Rosenzweig, this infinitization of desire is at bottom an affirmation of a fundamental *impasse*, a refusal to compromise with respect to a hindrance internal to its desire. And concerning the no-

29. See Richard Wagner, *Stories and Essays*, ed. Charles Osborne (LaSalle, Ill.: Open Court, 1991), 23–39.

30. In Levinas's rather more lyrical terms, this infinitization of desire rehearsed not only in Judaism but also in, of all places, Descartes's *Meditations*, can be understood as the intromission of the Infinite into a finite human consciousness: "The *in* of Infinite designates the depth of the affecting by which subjectivity is affected through this 'putting' of the Infinite into it, without prehension or comprehension. It designates the depth of an undergoing that no capacity comprehends, that no foundation any longer supports, where every process of investing fails. . . . This putting in without a corresponding recollecting devastates its site like a devouring fire, catastrophying its site. . . . The negativity of the *in* of the Infinite—otherwise than being, divine comedy—hollows out a desire which cannot be filled, nourishes itself with its very augmentation, and is exalted as a desire, withdraws from its satisfaction in the measure that it approaches the desirable. It is a desire that is beyond satisfaction, and, unlike a need, does not identify a term or an end." Levinas, *Basic Philosophical Writings*, 139.

tion of Hebrew as neither a living nor a dead language but rather as a *holy* language, Rosenzweig writes: "The holiness of the people's own language has an effect similar to that of the holiness of its own land: it does not allow all their feeling to be lavished on everyday life. It prevents the eternal people from ever being quite in harmony with the times" (301). The Jews are, in this view, fundamentally out of joint with respect to the socio-symbolic relations that constitute the lives, the being-in-history, of other peoples and nations.

Correlative to this "out-of-jointness" is the turn toward what Rosenzweig, in what for many readers is understandably his most disturbing claim about the Jews and Judaism, refers to as "the community of blood": "This [infinitized] longing compels it to concentrate the full force of its will on a thing which, for other peoples, is only one among others yet which to it is essential and vital: the community of blood" (300). It should, however, be clear that this is not an argument for a distinctive genetic or racial quality to Jewish blood; the claim is rather that Jewish self-preservation takes place above all in and through reproduction and family rather than through territory, architecture, state institutions, or armies. When Rosenzweig speaks of blood he thus ultimately means that family is the primary site of the *memic*—rather than *genetic*—replication of Judaism.[31] The collective will of the Jews, however, thereby assumes the dimension of a *tautology:* "the will to be a people dares not cling to any mechanical means; the will can realize its end only through the people itself" [*"das Volk ist Volk nur durch das Volk"*] (300).

Here Rosenzweig is in effect reproducing the argument he made about the metaethical self only now with respect to the Jews as a collective. Like the metaethical self, which also assumed the form of a tautology—$B = B$—the Jews are for Rosenzweig the people

---

31.   See Jan Assmann's brilliant discussion of Deuteronomy as a paradigm of cultural mnemotechnics in his *Das kulturelle Gedächtnis. Schrift, Erinnerung und politische Identität in frühen Hochkulturen* (Munich: C. H. Beck, 1997). There Assmann argues that it is precisely the mnemotechnical procedures elaborated in Deuteronomy, procedures that make superfluous the "natural" frameworks and supports of collective and cultural memory—territory, temple, monarchy—that allowed for the survival of the Jews in the diaspora. In effect, these procedures constitute the Jews as a people whose foundational *"lieux de mémoire"* are uncoupled from territory, architecture, and political institutions. Rosenzweig's point is basically that the primary social site of Jewish cultural mnemotechnics is the family.

whose life is focused not on its *predicative being*, but rather on what remains in excess of, what persists beyond, the predicates that distinguish a historical people from other historical peoples. Jewish difference—and here Freud and Rosenzweig are in agreement—is not to be located at the level of distinctive national predicates—the level of historical particularity—but rather at the level of a singular, meta-historical destiny that, much like the metaethical self, has its own "birthday," an eventful emergence proper to it.[32] For both Freud and Rosenzweig, Jewish difference and survival is linked not to any special talents or properties but rather to the enigma of election that opens on to an order of experience "beyond the pleasure principle," beyond the teleological strivings that constitute the historical life of nations. As Rosenzweig would later put it, "There is no *essence*—that would be 'concept'—of Judaism. There is only a 'Hear O Israel.'"[33]

Pursuing the homology between meta-historical destiny and metaethical selfhood can help us further. The latter, as we saw, cannot be understood as some sort of "true self" beyond the life of the personality. In the same way, to be the subject of meta-historical rupture cannot mean simply to be placed outside of history, as if history

---

32. The status of this second birth allows Rosenzweig to distinguish Judaism and Christianity in a novel way. For the Jews, the second birth takes place prior to the birth of the Jewish individual; for Christians, the second birth must be experienced by each Christian individually: "The rebirth of the Jew . . . is not his personal one, but the transformation of his people for freedom in the divine covenant of revelation. On that occasion the people experienced a second birth, and he in it, not he personally as an individual. . . . The decisive moment, the great Now, the miracle of rebirth, lies before the individual life. . . . It is just the contrary with the Christian. In his personal life there occurs to him at a given point the miracle of rebirth, and it occurs to him as an individual." *Star*, 396. This accounts for the different spiritual "characters" of the two formations: "The individual Jew generally lacks that personal vitality which only comes to a man in the second birth, with the 'intrusion of the self.' For although the [Jewish] people has the defiantly demonic self in full measure, the individual [Jew] has it not at all. Rather he is from his first birth on whatever he is as Jew, in a sense, then by virtue of his personality, not of his character. Correspondingly, the Christian loses everything 'natural,' everything innate, in his Christianity. . . . They [Christians] are relieved of being-Christian before birth by the birth of Christ, just as, contrariwise, the Jew is relieved of becoming-Jew in the protohistory of his people's revelation, while he possesses his being Jew in himself from birth on and carries it with him." Ibid., 396–97.

33. Franz Rosenzweig, *Der Mensch und sein Werk. Gesammelte Schriften*, ed. Reinhold Mayer and Annemarie Mayer (Dordrecht: Martinus Nijhoff, 1984), 3:601.

were some sort of container beyond which one could still structure a life. But nor can it mean that the Jews simply have—or rather *had*—their elected "part" to play in some larger "whole" of History whose meaning would eventually become manifest. That is precisely the Hegelian concept of the destiny of nations in opposition to which Rosenzweig posits the singularity of Jewish election. Both of these views—that Jewish life is played out outside the frame of history; that Jewish life plays its part within a larger whole of History— can be deemed *metaphysical* in that they are committed to a picture of the world and of history as *a delimited domain* of some sort. In Rosenzweig's terms, they are pictures generated by the "old thinking." From the perspective of the "new thinking," Jewish destiny is neither simply *historical* nor simply *ahistorical*, that is, neither simply apart from nor merely contained within the rhythms of world history, but rather *meta-historical*, articulated with the remnants *immanent* to history.[34]

It is in this spirit that I read Rosenzweig's discussion of the prophetic notion of the "remnant of Israel." "In defiance of all secular history," Rosenzweig writes, "Jewish history is the history of the remnant; the word of the prophet, that it 'will remain,' ever applies to it" (404). Rosenzweig goes on to link the logic of the remnant to the notion of contraction:

> All secular history deals with expansion. Power is the basic
> concept of history because in Christianity revelation began to

---

34.   In an essay on the concept of *home*, Bonnie Honig has offered a vision of social democratic politics as, precisely, fidelity to such remnants or remainders. See "Difference, Dilemmas, and the Politics of Home," in *Democracy and Difference. Contesting the Boundaries of the Political*, ed. Seyla Benhabib (Princeton: Princeton University Press, 1996), 257–77. The problem, of course, is how one understands these remnants. Honig posits them as indices of the very sort of difference that Rosenzweig links to the Judaic innovation: "Recent work in political and feminist theory . . . suggest that difference is not simply a different identity, nor is it merely (*pace* Hegel) the constitutive matter out of which identity is formed; it is also that which resists or exceeds the closure of identity. It signals not a difference *from* others but a difference that troubles identity from with*in* its would-be economy of the same. Difference is what identity perpetually seeks (and fails) to expunge, fix, or hold in place. In short, difference is a problem for identity, not one of its adjectives." Ibid., 257–58. Difference and, thus, the remnant are not, that is, to be located at the level of the *predicative being* of individuals or collectives. I return to the political dimension of the remnant at the end of this chapter.

spread over the world, and thus every expansionist urge, even that which consciously was purely secular, became the unconscious servant of this expansionist movement. But Judaism, and it alone in all the world, maintains itself by subtraction, by contraction, by the formation of ever new remnants. . . . In Judaism, man is always somehow a survivor, an inner something, whose exterior was seized by the current of the world and carried off while he himself, what is left of him, remains standing on the shore. Something within him is waiting. (404–5)[35]

From a Rosenzweigian perspective, Freud's error in *Moses and Monotheism* was to reduce this *logic of the remnant* that he, too, discerned in the Jewish *Gestalt* to the "stuckness" of an obsessive-compulsive pathology based on an unconfessed feeling of guilt. Rosenzweig's argument in the *Star* allows us to understand Jewish "stuckness"—his wartime correspondence with Eugen Rosenstock revolved in large part around the thought of Jewish *Verstocktheit*[36]—not, or at least not simply, as the unredeemed hauntedness pertaining to the violence of ethnogenetic foundations but rather as placeholder, as mode of appearance, of a certain *rupture* with the time and space of ethnic and national histories. There is, of course, something defiant or even "demonic" about this rupture and it is no doubt the force of this defiance that stands behind Walter Benjamin's difficult notion of *"göttliche Gewalt"* or divine violence. Freud's error

35.   In his discussion of the mystical doctrine of the Shekhina, Rosenzweig gives the logic of the remnant a quasi-excremental cast that really only comes through in the German: "For the sufferings of this remnant, the constant requirement to separate and exclude oneself [*das ständige Sichscheiden und Sichausscheidenmüssen*], all this now becomes a suffering for God's sake, and the remnant is the bearer of this suffering." *Star*, 410. In this context we might recall Žižek's suggestion that one of the differences between Foucault's understanding of the post-Kantian subject and Lacan's is that the former is "synonymous with . . . successful subjectivization, with the formation of the self *qua* an esthetic whole" whereas the "Lacanian subject is synomymous with its failure, i.e., it is correlative to the anal object, to the excrement which is the leftover of every subjectivization." Slavoj Žižek, *Enjoy Your Symptom! Jacques Lacan in Hollywood and Out* (London: Routledge, 1992), 183–84.

36.   See Eugen Rosenstock-Huessy, ed., *Judaism Despite Christianity: The "Letters on Christianity and Judaism" between Eugen Rosenstock-Huessy and Franz Rosenzweig* (New York: Schocken, 1971).

was to equate it with a specifically Jewish cultivation of the superego. Rosenzweig, for his part, makes a compelling case that it must rather be understood as a conversion or unplugging from the "normal" ways of *succumbing* to superego pressure, of remaining addicted to the repetition compulsions—the "Egyptomaniacal" labors—that sustain idolatrous attachments.

Here we might recall Giorgio Agamben's remarks apropos of the man from the country in Kafka's parable, "Before the Law." The point of the parable is not simply to illustrate the petitioner's capture by the law—*The Trial*, the novel in which the parable appears, is itself a brilliant elaboration of the superego dynamic involved in this capture—but also to allegorize the nature of the messianic task, namely, the suspension of that very dynamic, the interruptive bringing to light of the law's traumatic "foundation" in an excess of validity over meaning.

If there is a "messianic politics" in Judaism it derives, Rosenzweig suggests, from its refusal to transfer the energies of superego to the ultimately defensive national projects that organize the lives and homelands of other historical peoples and political communities. In a certain sense, then, Freud's emphasis on the connection between Judaism and superego is not at all wrong; we might even say that the superego is at some level born with Judaism, first comes to light with it as a palpable and disturbing entity, is first *revealed* there as the very kernel of the discontent that haunts civilization. Freud and Rosenzweig are, then, in agreement that Judaism distinguishes itself by, as it were, *refusing to exorcise these ghosts* (therein lies the signficance of the Jewish turn from practices of sorcery, magic, necromancy).

The tension between the Freudian and Rosenzweigian view with respect to the superego can be seen to revolve around the two kinds or aspects of interpellation to which I have referred at various places in this book. Here Žižek's remarks about the difference between the senses of "subjectivization" in the work of Alain Badiou and Ernesto Laclau are instructive: "[F]or Badiou, subjectivization designates the event of Truth that disrupts the closure of the hegemonic ideological domain and/or the existing social edifice (the Order of Being); while for Laclau, the gesture of subjectivization is the very gesture of establishing a (new) hegemony, and is as such the elementary gesture of ideology."[37] What both Freud and Rosenzweig suggest—though each places the emphasis differently—is that Judaism emerges at the intersection of these two senses of "subjectivization." What comes to light in the "Truth-Event" of revelation is, in some sense, nothing but the ways in which the "Order of Being," the order of third-personal relations, captures or "undeadens" the subject. By, as it were, turning us toward this undeadness, *calling us to accept responsibility for it*, revelation opens up the possibility of converting what had functioned as a support of ideological captivation into a locus of suspension and interruption. Revelation converts the "surplus cause" of our relational surrender, our passionate attachments to ideological formations—our various forms of *idolatry*—into a "remnant" of them.[38]

VI

The ethical dimension of such a conversion transpires, as I have been emphasizing, in the opening to and acknowledgment of the Other qua *stranger*; the Other whose face manifests the "spectral aura" of an unassumable *jouissance*.[39] In the *Star*, Rosenzweig argues that such an acknowledgment of the Other must, in turn, be sustained by a form of life, by a shape of human collectivity. For Rosenzweig, the communities established in and through revelation are paradoxical in that they are constituted, from the start, in relation to the remnant, that is, to a hindrance to or leftover of the very forms

---

37. Slavoj Žižek, *The Ticklish Subject. The Absent Center of Political Ontology* (London: Verso, 1999), 183.

38. Leora Batnitzky has placed the critique of idolatry at the very center of Rosenzweig's project. See Batnitzky, *Idolatry and Representation. The Philosophy of Franz Rosenzweig Reconsidered* (Princeton: Princeton University Press, 2000).

39. As Derrida, too, has underlined, the strangeness of the stranger cannot be captured by any ethnic, national, or cultural predicate: "And the other is not reducible to its actual predicates, to what one might define or thematize about it, anymore than the I is. It is naked, bared of every property, and this nudity is also its infinitely exposed vulnerability: its skin. This absence of determinable properties, of concrete predicates, of empirical visibility, is no doubt what gives to the face of the other a spectral aura." Jacques Derrida, *Adieu. To Emmanuel Levinas*, trans. Pascale-Anne Brault and Michael Naas (Stanford: Stanford University Press, 1999), 111.

of identification that normally sustain the psychic bonds of communities. As Levinas has put it:

> The Torah is transcendent and from heaven by its demands
> *that clash, in the final analysis, with the pure ontology of the world.*
> The Torah demands, in opposition to the natural perseverance
> of each being in his or her own being (a fundamental ontological law), concern for the stranger, the widow and orphan, a
> preoccupation with the other person.[40]

Though he says little about this in the *Star*, in the years following its composition Rosenzweig clearly came to believe more and more that these "demands" could not be abstracted from the multiplicity of commandments that make up *halakhah*, the life of normative Judaism. In contrast to his more famous friend and interlocutor on these matters, Martin Buber, he came to feel that it was precisely in and through these commandments that Judaism lives its rupture with the "pure ontology of the world," cultivates its assumption of responsibility for the remnant.[41] The commandments, in this view, serve to elaborate for everyday life the relevant "concept" of the Other and of the Other's claims on us, that is to say, the forms of acknowledgment owed an Other whose alterity bears witness to the fact of his or her exposure to an excess of validity over meaning immanent to the "ontology of the world." What makes Judaism different is that it elaborates a form of life around the disruptive, even traumatic, pressures induced in us by the "neighbor-Thing" rather than, under the auspices of the superego, transferring those pressures into this or that national project, this or that construction of "home" (it ought, thus, to be very clear why Rosenzweig could never

---

40.   Quoted in ibid., 123.

41.   Arguing against Buber's privileging of the I–Thou relation over and against Jewish law, Rosenzweig suggests, in an open letter to him in 1923, that Buber's conception of the commandments was overly influenced by nineteenth-century neo-Orthodoxy. "Is that really Jewish law, the law of millennia, studied and lived, analyzed and rhapsodized, the law of everyday and of the day of death, petty and yet sublime, sober and yet woven in legend; a law which knows both the fire of the Sabbath candle and that of the martyr's stake?" See Franz Rosenzweig, "The Builders," in *Franz Rosenzweig. His Life and Thought*, ed. Nahum Glatzer (Indianapolis: Hackett, 1998), 237–38. It is precisely this intersection of the "petty" and the "sublime" that marks what I have been referring to as the *midst of life*.

become a Zionist in any recognizable sense of that term).[42] We might say, then, that the commandments come to frame, for Rosenzweig, the form of life correlative to the philosophical method he had employed in the *Star* and the "new thinking," more generally, a method he referred to as *absolute empiricism:* attunement to the surplus of the real within reality.[43]

Rosenzweig develops his thinking about this correlation—his conception of the performance of the commandments as the everyday life of "absolute empiricism," attunement to the Other in his or her uncanny singularity—in a letter written in November 1924 to his colleagues at the *Jüdisches Lehrhaus* in Frankfurt. There Rosenzweig once more takes up Buber's challenge regarding Jewish law, a challenge that can be expressed in the thought "that only the election of the people of Israel came from God, but that all the details of the Law came from man alone."[44] As Richard Cohen has put it in a compelling reading of the letter, "Rosenzweig attempts to make the external connection revelation-election and law an internal one. Revelation, being loved, entails more than a blanket imperative to love the neighbor; it requires, *as can only be experienced from within,* that the Jew follow the individual commandments of the Jewish law, mitzvot."[45] Rosenzweig himself formulates this connection in terms that recall Kafka's short prose text "The Top," which we considered at the beginning of chapter 1. In the immediacy of the theo-human reality of the commandments, Rosenzweig writes,

42.   Rosenzweig wrote in 1917 that "[i]t is only by keeping their ties to the Diaspora that the Zionists will be forced to keep their eyes on the goal, which is to become stateless inside time, and to remain nomads, even over there [in Palestine]." Quoted in Stéphane Mosès, *System and Revelation. The Philosophy of Franz Rosenzweig,* trans. Catherine Tihanyi (Detroit: Wayne State University Press, 1992), 207.

43.   I am referring, once more, to Rosenzweig's formulation in his essay, "The New Thinking," in *New Thinking,* 101. In the *Star,* Rosenzweig writes that in the morning prayers on the Sabbath "we find utterance of the people's awareness of being elect through the gift of the Torah which signifies that eternal life has been planted in their midst." *Star,* 312. We might also hear this to mean that with the gift of the Torah man is eternally planted in the *midst of life,* in proximity to the surplus of the real in reality.

44.   Quoted in *Franz Rosenzweig,* ed. Glatzer, 242. Subsequent references are to "*Lehrhaus* letter." In the letter, Rosenzweig attributes the formulation to Glatzer and further identifies it as his own problematic position, though it is clearly Buber's view.

45.   Richard A. Cohen, *Elevations. The Height of the Good in Rosenzweig and Levinas* (Chicago: University of Chicago Press, 1994), 37; emphasis added.

we may not "express" God [*Gott aussprechen*], but rather address God [*Gott ansprechen*] in the individual commandment. For whoever seeks to express him will discover that he who cannot be expressed will become he who cannot be found. Only in the commandment can the voice of him who commands be heard. . . . Not that doing necessarily results in hearing and understanding. But one hears differently when one hears in the doing.[46]

One cannot, in other words, grasp the meaning of a concept—in this instance, Jewish election—in abstraction from the practices and experiences in which that concept has its life. As Cohen puts it, "what is experienced and what can be stated objectively are not coextensive."[47]

To make his point more concrete, Rosenzweig cites the example of a marriage:

What we can thus state—or even prove—about God is related to our possible "experience" in the same way that the empty announcement that two persons have married, or the showing of the marriage certificate, is related to the daily and hourly reality of this marriage. The reality cannot be communicated to a third person; it is no one's concern and yet it is the only thing that counts, and the objective statement of the fact of marriage would be meaningless without this most private, incommunicable reality. And so even the bare fact of marriage does not become real save where it leaves the sphere of what can be objectively stated and enters the secret pale of the festive days and anniversaries of private life.[48]

We might also add: the secret pale of eccentricities and perversities that constitute the psychopathology of the everyday life of marriage. In light of the larger significance of Rosenzweig's example—the relationship between God and Israel has traditionally been allegorized as that of a husband and wife—the commandments, especially the

46. *Lehrhaus* letter, 245–46.
47. Cohen, *Elevations*, 36.
48. *Lehrhaus* letter, 243.

ones that strike the outsider as being utterly irrational and nonsensical, thereby assume the further aspect of the absolutely singular way in which a couple shapes their "impossible" life together. Every couple's life is structured around a set of shared and often nonsensical rules and patterns that they would never admit to an outsider. Rosenzweig's claim is, at some level, that one cannot simply throw out this dirty bath water without also losing the baby—the functioning of the marriage.

Rosenzweig refuses, then, to engage in any rational reconstruction of halakhic life. Indeed, he characterizes the pressure to produce such a reconstruction as a source of pain and humiliation that post-Enlightenment Jewry has all too blindly accepted: "From Mendelssohn on, our entire people has subjected itself to the torture of this embarrassing questioning; the Jewishness of every individual has squirmed on the needle point of a 'why.'"[49] Rosenzweig's point about the commandments is at least in part that they serve to *sustain* the enigma of election as a vital experience rather than allowing it to be translated into a "why" question, a question available to sociological, historical, or even psychoanalytic explanation. However, given the "internal" connection now posited between the multiplicity of commandments, on the one hand, and the hospitality toward the "neighbor-Thing" that continues to constitute the heart of revelation, on the other, the claim must be, nonetheless, that what one hears in the doing, in the obeying of the commandments, attunes the hearer to a more emphatic sense, an infinitely more demanding aspect, of what it means to be in the midst of life: to be subject to the presence of the singular Other, the multifarious ways in which I am called upon to acknowledge and to respond to this uncanny presence. The force of the commandments derive, in other words, not simply from the fact that they permeate the practices of everyday life (rather than present a series of principles or theological doctrines about man, God, and world), but also from the fact that they emphatically turn the one thereby engaged *to* everyday life and the Other who is there with us. In the life shaped by the commandments there is always this stranger in our midst.

This means, however, that Judaism cannot be understood

49.   Rosenzweig, "The Builders," 238.

simply as another culture, another form of life, defined by the practices and traditions that give every culture its depth and richness. The dense "materiality" of the life elaborated in the commandments is, in other words, of a different order than that of the embodied practices one finds in every culture and that is available to anthropological thick description. It is a materiality not of an *embodied ethos* but rather of the *metaethical remnant,* a materiality correlative, that is, to that of the "Neighbor-Thing." This also means that the hospitality at stake in this paradoxical "form of life" cannot be understood in the "tribal" sense, that is, as the sort of ritualized symbolic welcoming of the stranger that one finds in any number of cultures. The stranger in question in Judaism is, as I have been arguing, not the tribal stranger, the one who belongs to another culture or group to which one has obligations of hospitality, but rather the "monstrous" or "demonic" stranger who is also my neighbor. Again, the alterity in question here is not that of another ethos but rather of what is in excess of every ethos, every "tribal" identification.[50]

It is in this spirit that I also understand Rosenzweig's treatment of Jewish ritual in the *Star.* He characterizes the liturgical time established in and through ritual as one of the central ways in which Jews have traditionally anticipated a world of justice, a world open and hospitable to the stranger (a world where "neighbor" and "stranger" are no longer rigidly opposed). But as Rosenzweig would later emphasize in *Understanding the Sick and the Healthy,* the holiday "does not seek that which is absent from the work day, does not know what

---

50.   As Stéphane Mosès has put it, "This Law, with its meticulous precepts regulating all aspects of life, is a *praxis* turned toward the concrete reality of the world, but a praxis aiming at projecting into the world a transcendental order and meaning. In this sense the practice of the Law makes the 'world to come' appear in the midst of 'this world.'" Mosès, *System and Revelation,* 278. Nonetheless, the role of Jewish law in sustaining the kind of openness to the Other that we associate with the "world to come" and that was of primary interest to Rosenzweig remains a complex and deeply problematic one. Indeed, in the *Star,* Rosenzweig himself argues that the very way in which the Jews cultivate this openness has the potential to close them off from non-Jews. Jewish life, precisely as the life of the "remnant," is always, Rosenzweig suggests, haunted by the danger of "narrowness" and thus requires, as its necessary supplement with regard to its own redemptive vocation, the expansive love manifest in Christianity. For an extended and lucid discussion of the ways in which Rosenzweig elaborates this complex relation of mutual supplementarity between Judaism and Christianity, see Mosès, *System and Revelation.*

the work day is not capable of recognizing. It does, however, state explicitly and as a whole those things which the latter expresses only partially and occasionally." In that sense, the holiday can be seen as providing a kind of "training school for every day."[51] What distinguishes the holiday from the everyday is, as I have been arguing, precisely a certain *suspension of fantasy*—call it the exodus or Sabbath from the "Egyptomania" that burdens everyday life, constrains our capacities to respond to the Other—rather than some sort of escape from the ordinary into a wish-fulfilling realm of fantasy or ecstatic "state of exception." Such an exodus or Sabbath, thus, points not to a new and completely different life elsewhere but rather to the "small adjustment" which, as Benjamin suggests in his essay on Kafka, opens us to new possibilities of community *here and now*. Apropos of the figure of *"Das bucklicht Männlein"* ["The Little Hunchback"], that prototype of burdened, "undeadened" life, Benjamin writes, "This little man is at home in distorted life [*ist der Insasse des entstellten Lebens*]; he will disappear with the coming of the Messiah, of whom a great rabbi once said that he did not wish to change the world by force, but would only make a slight adjustment in it."[52]

None of this should be taken to mean, however, that Rosenzweig is staking a claim for some sort of absolute priority for this form of life, that it is, in other words, *only* by virtue of a life lived according to the commandments or structured around the rituals that punctuate the Jewish calender that one can truly inhabit the midst of life and that all other forms are to be understood as deficient, as "defenses" of one sort or another. Indeed, in his essay, "The New Thinking," Rosenzweig writes of the *Star* that "It is not a 'Jewish book' at all. . . ." Nor, he adds, does it "make the claim to be a philosophy of religion—how could it do that when the word 'religion' does not occur in it at all! Rather, it is merely a system of philosophy." Later in the same essay he addresses the seemingly privi-

51. Franz Rosenzweig, *Understanding the Sick and the Healthy. A View of World, Man, and God*, trans. Nahum Glatzer (Cambridge: Harvard University Press, 1999), 96, 99.

52. Walter Benjamin, "Franz Kafka. On the Tenth Anniversary of His Death," in *Illuminations*, trans. Harry Zohn (New York: Schocken, 1969), 134. This "great rabbi" refers, apparently, to none other than the young Gershom Scholem. I am grateful to Peter Fenves for alerting me to this bit of Benjaminian lore.

leged position of Judaism and Christianity in this system. "The extraordinary position of Judaism and Christianity lies," he writes, "precisely in that they, even when they have become religions, find in themselves the impulse to free themselves from this religiosity of theirs and to find their way back again to the open field of reality from out of their specialization and their fortification."[53]

Rosenzweig does, in the end, admit to a sense in which the *Star* might rightfully be regarded as a "Jewish book," but it is one that pertains to the historicity of all thinking—thinking that transpires in language—rather than to an eternal and privileged essence of "Judaism": "I received the new thinking in these old words, thus I have rendered it and passed it on, in them." It is, in other words, the force and efficacy of human speech—speech that is always of a time and place, that is always idiomatic—that makes the "parochialism" of the *Star* both possible and necessary:

> And yet this is a Jewish book: not one which deals with "Jewish matters," for then the books of the Protestant Old Testament scholars would be Jewish books, but one for which the

53.   Rosenzweig, "The New Thinking," 69, 91. In a diary entry from 1922 and one of the few places in his writings where Freud is explicitly cited, Rosenzweig even characterizes revelation as a kind of "anti-religion" aimed at loosening the grip of the "religionitis" that ensues when fantasmatic formations or "totems" of any kind begin to block our often anguished exposure to/answerability within the midst of life. See Franz Rosenzweig, *Der Mensch und sein Werk: Gesammelte Schriften*, ed. Rachel Rosenzweig and Edith Rosenzweig-Scheinmann (The Hague: Martinus Nijhoff, 1974–84), vol. 1, part 2, 770–71.

In much the same spirit, I think, Derrida has spoken of a "structural messianicity," one dissociated "from every determinate messianism: a messianicity before or without any messianism incorporated by some revelation in a determined place that goes by the name of Sinai or Mount Horeb." Derrida, *Adieu*, 118–19. In another effort at characterizing this notion, Derrida's language resonates with what I have been calling the "psychotheology of everyday life": "Messianicity (which I regard as a universal structure of experience, and which cannot be reduced to religious messianism of any stripe) is anything but Utopian: it refers, in every here-and-now, to the coming of an eminently real, concrete event, that is, to the most irreducibly heterogeneous otherness. Nothing is more 'realistic' or 'immediate' than this messianic apprehension, straining forward toward the event of him who/that which is coming. . . . This is an ineluctability whose imperative, always here-and-now, in singular fashion, can in no case yield to the allure of Utopia, at least not to what the word literally signifies or is ordinarily taken to mean." Jacques Derrida, "Marx and Sons," in *Ghostly Demarcations: A Symposium on Jacques Derrida's Specters of Marx*, ed. Michael Sprinker (London: Verso, 1999), 248–49.

old Jewish words come in order to say what it has to say, and precisely for the new things it has to say. Jewish matters are, as matters generally are, always already past; but Jewish words, even if old, take part in the eternal youth of the word, and if the world is opened to them, then they will renew the world.[54]

VII

The *Star*, as these last remarks indicate, is concerned not only with the event of revelation; it is ultimately concerned with the ways in which human beings, alone and in collectives, move out into the world, into relations of production and exchange, *on behalf of revelation*. This movement constitutes *the work of redemption* and the last volume of the *Star* focuses exclusively on the ways in which this work shapes the life of the religious communities—Judaism and Christianity—to which Rosenzweig was historically and existentially linked. I conclude this chapter by exploring the broader implications of what Rosenzweig says here for contemporary theories of political community.

To put it in the terms of recent political debates, I would say that for Rosenzweig, the work of redemption to which both religious communities are, in his view, dedicated, pertains to the process of *universalization* in contrast to that of *globalization*. More specifically, it pertains to a mode of *subjectification*—Rosenzweig's term is *Beseelung* or ensoulment—on the basis of a logic of remnants immanent to the historical dynamic of globalization. That is the dynamic that Rosenzweig understood as the expansion and ramification of the third-personal relations of production and exchange within which human beings assume their social identities, their predicative being. The Kingdom of God is, in other words, not to be conceived as some sort of final inscription/integration of all subjects into a global totality but rather as *the infinite verification of the dimension of singularity* opened in revelatory love.[55] In Rosenzweig's terms, love introduces

---

54. Rosenzweig, "The New Thinking," 92.

55. Once again, Rosenzweig was committed to the view that Judaism and Christianity were deeply linked precisely by way of the *differences* in their modes of "verification."

the dimension of the *proper name* into the world of things, or rather, the proper name holds the place of that which remains in excess of our inscription into the part–whole logic of any totality:

> With the summons of the proper name, the word of revelation entered the real dialogue. With the proper name, the rigid wall of objectness has been breached. That which has a name of its own can no longer be a thing, no longer everyman's af-fair. It is incapable of utter absorption into the category [*er ist unfähig, restlos in die Gattung einzugehen*] for there can be no category for it to belong to; it is its own category. Nor does it still have its place in the world, its moment in occurrence. Rather it carries its here and now with it. Wherever it is, there is a midpoint and wherever it opens its mouth, there is a begin-ning. (186–87)

And as Rosenzweig indicates, the impact of this "beginning" is al-ways disruptive, even anarchic, from the perspective of the third-personal relations organizing our predicative being: "True it [the world qua order of part–whole relations] sees that something is hap-pening here . . . but not what is happening: the ensouling vivification [*Durchseelung*] of the growing life of the world. This occurrence is invisible from the vantage point of the world. Thus it only sees an-archy, disorder, interruption of its quietly growing life" (239).

In a recent book on the notion of political dispute, Jacques Rancière has reserved the term *police order* for the world of part–whole relations, for the social body subdivided into parts, and *politics* for the interruptive gesture that opens the dimension of universality on the basis of that which finds no place within these subdivisions, the remainder of this fundamentally arithmetic operation.[56] Ran-cière traces the historical possibility of this gesture, which allows for the "appearance"—we might say, revelation—of the Universal in and through the Global, to the emergence of Athenian democracy understood as the moment when the part of society that had no share

---

56. Jacques Rancière, *Disagreement. Politics and Philosophy*, trans. Julie Rose (Minneapolis: University of Minnesota Press, 1999). Subsequent references are given in the text.

in its wealth and power identified itself with the community as a whole:

> The people are nothing more than the undifferentiated mass of those who have no positive qualification—no wealth, no virtue—but who are nonetheless acknowledged to enjoy the same freedom as those who do. . . . The demos attributes to itself as its proper lot the equality that belongs to all citizens. In so doing, this party that is not one identifies its improper property with the exclusive principle of community and identifies its name—the name of the indistinct mass of men of no position—with the name of the community itself. . . . On top of this, it is through the existence of this part of those who have no part, of this nothing that is all, that the community exists as a political community—that is, as divided by a fundamental dispute, by a dispute to do with the counting of the community's parts even more than of their "rights." The people are not one class among others. They are the class of the wrong that harms the community and establishes it as a "community" of the just and the unjust. (8–9)

Politics, in other words, is the emergence of a conflict between two logics of being-together, one that pertains to "the distribution of places and roles . . . and the systems for legitimizing this distribution" (28), and another that pertains to "the equality, neither arithmetical nor geometric, of *any speaking beings whatsoever*" (28; emphasis added). We might refer to this second logic as one pertaining to the *pronomial being*—in contrast to the *predicative being*—of human life. The act of universalization/politicization is a specific and local dramatization of the tension of these logics. One "politicizes" a wrong, a miscount in the distribution of places and roles, by allowing it to stand in for a symptomatic torsion of the entire system of distribution and apportionment. In this way one opens the possibility of reconfiguring the space in which parts and roles are assigned. In terms of Freud's topography of the mind, if the superego is the psychic agency that polices our identity, our part or place within a whole, then it can now also be understood as the agency that constrains our capacity for just such acts of politicization.

A dramatic performance of such a gesture of universalization/

politicization took place in the final days of the German Democratic Republic when, during the demonstrations against the regime, the crowds began to chant *"Wir sind das Volk"* ("We are the People"). In Rancière's terms, the moment this performative contradiction mutated into the demand for quick reunification with the West—*"Wir sind ein Volk"* ("We are *One* People")—politics became reabsorbed into the police order, the arithmetic labor of apportioning parts and roles according to the perceived necessities of the global market system. What was lost thereby was not merely some fantasy of a "third path" between market capitalism and state socialism but rather the very space of political dispute, that is, the possibility of intervening precisely into this *perception of necessity*. As Rancière puts it, "politics exists wherever the count of parts and parties of society is disturbed by the inscription of a part of those who have no part. . . . Politics ceases wherever this gap no longer has any place, wherever the whole of the community is reduced to the sum of its parts *with nothing left over*" (123; emphasis added).[57]

Rosenzweig's conception of Jewish *"Verstocktheit"* or implacability, which Freud diagnosed as a form of obsessive-compulsive neurosis, is precisely an embodied insistence on this gap, on the disruptive leftover in the count of the community's parts and thus on the hope for a politics beyond the "police order." We might even say that Rosenzweig's notion of the "fire" at the heart of the "star of redemption" is nothing but the cultivation—in rite, commandment, and thought—of the *state of emergence* of this gap/remnant.[58] It is

57. In a commentary on Rancière, Žižek argues that this collapse of the dimension of politics proper defines even the tolerant liberal attitude that tries to account for the specific injuries suffered by infinitely subdividable subject groups ("not only homosexuals but African-American lesbians, African-American lesbian mothers, African-American unemployed lesbian mothers . . . "). What gets lost in such a procedure, Žižek writes, "is the gesture of *politicization* proper: although the difficulties of being an African-American unemployed lesbian mother are adequately catalogued right down to its most specific features, the concerned subject none the less somehow 'feels' that there is something 'wrong' and 'frustrating' in this very effort to mete out justice to her specific predicament—what she is deprived of is the possibility of 'metaphoric' elevation of her specific 'wrong' into a stand-in for the universal 'wrong.'" Žižek, *Ticklish Subject*, 203–4.

58. Rosenzweig characterizes Judaism as the "fire" and Christianity as the "rays" of the star of redemption.

in this spirit that I understand Rosenzweig's characterization of the absoluteness of Jewish self-positing, of Judaism's self-understanding not as a nation or cultural identity among others, but rather as a *singular universal*, one in which differences are, as it were, *taken inside* rather than posited as external, as differences from diverse and multiple Others (this is not, that is, an argument about *cultural pluralism*):

> The very difference of an individual people from other peoples establishes its connection with them. There are two sides to every boundary. By setting separating borders for ourselves, we border on something else. By being an individual people, a nation becomes a people among others. To close oneself off is to come close to another. *But this does not hold when a people refuses to be merely an individual people and wants to be "the one people."* Under these circumstances it must not close itself off within borders, but include within itself such borders as would, through their double function, tend to make it one individual people among others. And the same is true of its God, man, and world. These three must likewise not be distinguished from those of others; their distinction must be included within its own borders. (305–6; emphasis added)

In this view, Jewish "identity" emerges where the remnant posits itself as "the name of the community itself."[59] Judaism embodies, in other words, a certain refusal to accept the social body divided into parts, this partition of the perceptible, *as being all.* The logic of "non-all" cultivated within Judaism points, however, not to an Elsewhere outside of history, at the "end of the world" (beyond the false totality of existing social reality); it rather calls into question our defenses against the deeply political dimension of our life *in history.*

What I have up to now characterized as defenses against the ethical encounter with our neighbor must be amplified; what is at issue here are always at some level defenses against the encounter with our neighbor in the singular way in which he or she is *caught in*

---

59.   In Rancière's terms, "The difference that political disorder inscribes in the police order can . . . be expressed as the difference between subjectification and identification. It inscribes a subject name as being different from any identified part of the community." Rancière, *Disagreement*, 37.

the miscount, in the tension of logics, at the heart of society (it might be more accurate to say, the singular way in which human beings live their oblivion to this miscount, are "undeadened" by it). The Other's enigma, the claims the Other makes upon me in and through the disorders of his or her desire, always in some sense pertain to this double inscription; we belong not only to the order of third-personal relations of exchange—the part–whole logic of the social body, the order of "globalization"—but also to the dialogical space of encounter (potentially) opened on the basis of remnants ineluctably produced by that order. As Rancière puts it, "Political impropriety is not not belonging. It is belonging twice over: belonging to the world of properties and parts and belonging to the improper community, to that community that egalitarian logic sets up as the part of those who have no part" (137). The work of redemption is, we might say, the universalization of that improper community. And if Rancière finally adds that this "place of . . . impropriety is not exile," is "not the beyond where the human, in all its nakedness, would confront itself or its other, monster and/or divinity" (137), we ought to read these words not as a critique of Rosenzweig's more "psychotheological" approach to these same concerns but rather as consonant with the very words with which he ends the *Star*. For the fundamental concern in this approach has been, all along, the possibility of truly inhabiting the *midst of life*:

> To walk humbly with thy God—the words are written over
> the gate, the gate which leads out of the mysterious-
> miraculous light of the divine sanctuary in which no man can
> remain alive. Whither then, do the wings of the gate open?
> Thou knowest not? INTO LIFE. (424)

What Remains

I

In these final pages, I would like to address very briefly Rosenzweig's understanding of the work of redemption—the movement outward into the world on behalf of revelatory love—in the context of *aesthetic* artifacts whose importance to Rosenzweig, and indeed to his entire generation, is well known: the poetry of Friedrich Hölderlin. These brief remarks on poetry are warranted not only on the basis of Rosenzweig's particular relationship to Hölderlin's work and to the "Idealist" tradition to which it belongs, but also because of the crucial role played by art, poetry, and aesthetics in the *Star of Redemption*.

Rosenzweig's involvement with German Idealism was, as I have emphasized, deep and extensive. Not only did he publish a major dissertation on Hegel's political philosophy, he also edited and published an early document—really a kind of "manifesto"—of German Idealism under the title, "The Oldest Program of the System of German Idealism." Although Rosenzweig argued in the introductory essay that Schelling was the likely author of this unsigned text, scholars now generally agree that Hegel authored the manifesto in the context of intensive discussions with Hölderlin during their stay in Frankfurt in the mid-1790s. Without going into the discussion about authorship or the complex relation between the various parts of the manifesto—which deals with nothing less than the future of science, politics, ethics, art, religion, and education in the wake of the Enlightenment and the critical turn in philosophical thought inaugurated by Kant—it is nonetheless helpful here to quote what is no doubt one of the most striking formulations of the text and the one that most strongly resonates with Rosenzweig's understanding of the enduring *structural* tension between paganism and revelation:

> Monotheism of reason and the heart, polytheism of imagination and art, this is what we require! First I will speak of an idea which, as far as I know, has never occurred to anyone—we must have a new mythology, but this mythology must stand in the service of ideas, it must become a mythology of reason.[1]

This call for a new mythology is linked to the task of popularization, to the need to overcome the gap between educated and uneducated classes, intellectual elites and *das Volk*, by means of an aesthetic sublimation of the normative demands of theoretical and practical reason. Only an aesthetic philosophy, one guided by the idea of the *beautiful*, would have the power to induct all of humankind into the realm of freedom and equality, the demands of which are perforce experienced as excessively abstract and formal, that is, as unsustainable demands for abstraction and formalization in the pursuit of truth and the good.[2] This new philosophy—the aesthetic form of which would have to be, according to the manifesto, that of a mythology

---

1. Quoted in *Mythologie der Vernunft. Hegels 'ältestes Systemprogramm' des deutschen Idealismus*, ed. Christoph Jamme and Helmut Schneider (Frankfurt am Main: Suhrkamp, 1984), 13.

2. Whoever finally authored this manifesto, this appeal to the idea of the beautiful is doubtlessly indebted to the conception of beauty found in Hölderlin's novel *Hyperion*. This understanding of the pedagogical *uses* of beauty strongly resonate with eighteenth-century debates, especially in the context of freemasonry—one thinks, above all, of Mozart's *Magic Flute*—concerning the problem of *initiating* individuals and collectives into the austere universe of human reason.

of reason—is finally associated with expectations of a great religious awakening, the advent of the Johannine Age: "A higher spirit, sent from heaven, must establish this new religion among us; it will be the last great work of mankind."[3] Before turning to the specifically Hölderlinian dimension of this "great work," which I think we can only truly understand against the background of Rosenzweig's own project, I'd like to say a word about the status of aesthetics in the *Star* more generally.

II

In the *Star*, Rosenzweig correlates the central theological categories of the Judeo-Christian tradition—creation, revelation, and redemption—with aspects of the "life" of a work of art. In this schema, redemption is correlated with the reception of the work of art by an individual and, eventually, by a community that is in some sense constituted, called into being, by the work. In this view, a work finds its completion in acts of reception much as the world finds its fulfillment through the work of redemption, understood as the extension of God's revelation into the world through acts manifesting love of neighbor. But for Rosenzweig, a work's reception cannot be reduced to the unfolding of the inner logic of the work, the bringing to light of what is already in the work as a potential waiting to be actualized. In much the same way, it would be a mistake to understand revelation as a catalyst for the development of one's personality, the un-

---

3. *Systemprogramm*, 12. This notion of a final revelation that would serve to establish a fully spiritualized church, came, for the later Schelling, to be associated with the apocalyptic visions of John of Patmos, also the subject of one of Hölderlin's late hymns. On the relevance of all of this for Rosenzweig, Paul Mendes-Flohr has noted that the "eschatological hopes that German idealists associated with the Johannine form of Christianity were resonated anew by Rosenzweig and several other participants in the Baden-Baden conference of 1910—Rosenstock, Hans and Rudolf Ehrenberg—who together with others had founded in 1915 an informal group known as the Patmos circle." Mendes-Flohr goes on to cite a diary entry from 14 January 1916 in which Rosenzweig associates this new stage in world/Christian history with the World War: "the Johannine transformation of the Church brought about by the Enlightenment, has only become apparent in *this* war which embraces all of the Christian world and which is leading to supra-Christian politics." See Paul Mendes-Flohr, "Rosenzweig and the Crisis of Historicism," in *The Philosophy of Franz Rosenzweig*, ed. Paul Mendes-Flohr (Hanover, N.H.: University Press of New England, 1988), 146–47.

folding of one's talents and potentials, for "becoming who one is."[4] Rather, the act of reception, this *completion* of the work of art, represents a rupture in the life of the work—a "strong misreading" we might say—performed by one who feels singled out, addressed by it. By way of such an appropriation of the work in response to its singular mode of address, a work is endowed with a life beyond the order of knowledge, beyond a merely additive history of tastes and styles. Such "redemptive" reading can, to borrow the language of speech-act theory, never be reduced to a purely constative act of noting the positive features of the work but depends instead on a dimension of performativity.[5]

What makes a work of art inexhaustible, subject to multiple interpretations, is not simply an excess of content or information that, because of the limits of every human consciousness, requires multiple readings to "bring it out"; rather, this much noted inexhaustibility depends on the fact that every reading is, on a certain level, a kind of *creatio ex nihilo*. The details supporting a strong reading of a work only become visible retroactively, in light of the performative gesture that intervenes into its history of reception. In a certain sense, these details were not there before; they lacked ontological consistency. I am suggesting that the *Star* and Rosenzweig's "new thinking" more generally effectuates such a performative in-

4. Here one might recall from chapter 1 Rosenzweig's letter to Meinecke where what was at stake was precisely a break with the rule of the talents.

5. The *Star* suggests yet another way of understanding this performativity. A work of art is, as Rosenzweig emphasizes, without a home—is, as he puts it, *unheimlich*, uncanny: "The work of art stands there unique, detached from its originator, uncanny in its vitality which is full of life and yet alien to life. Yes, it is truly uncanny [*un-heimlich*]. It does not know the shelter of a category where it might nestle. It stands all by itself—a type to itself, a category to itself, not akin to any other thing, even to any other work of art." Franz Rosenzweig, *The Star of Redemption*, trans. William W. Hallo (Notre Dame: University of Notre Dame Press, 1985), 243. Subsequent references are given in the text. The act of reception is the act that gives this uncanny thing a place in life, a context. But the crucial point is that this act changes everything: the work as well as the life into which it has been "integrated"; in a sense, nothing remains the same. To miss this point is to confuse the reception of a work in this Rosenzweigian sense with some sort of reflection on or "cultural study" of the work, or, to use Barthes's terms, to collapse the response to the work's *punctum* into an elaboration of its *studium*. See Roland Barthes, *Camera Lucida. Reflections on Photography*, trans. Richard Howard (New York: Hill and Wang, 1981), 26.

tervention into the field of possibilities of reading Hölderlin, that Rosenzweig offers us a "lucky break" in our relationship to Hölderlin's work. In Walter Benjamin's terms, it is the shock of this performative gesture that crystallizes the work into a "monad," into the sign of a truth-event that can enter into—and alter the shape of—life and not simply into the order of positive knowledge (the order of part–whole, third-personal relations). Benjamin's dramatic language, offered as the key to a truly materialist engagement with the works of human culture, is well known. The historical materialist, Benjamin writes, takes cognizance of his subject "in order to blast a specific era out of the homogeneous course of history—blasting a specific life out of the era or a specific work out of the lifework." This destructive-constructive procedure is conceived as a mode of fidelity to what Benjamin refers to as "a Messianic cessation of happening" immanent in the work, the secular-political meaning of which is, as he puts it, "a revolutionary chance in the fight for the oppressed past."[6]

There has, of course, been much debate about the status of Friedrich Hölderlin's attachment to such revolutionary passions. This debate has often come down to the question whether he is above all a political poet or a religious one, whether he is a poet whose primary concern was with the structure of existing social relations or one whose mind and heart were absorbed by questions of divinity, of the nature of human-divine communication in the modern, "Hesperian," era. This debate can be understood as one concerning the specificity of Hölderlin's utopian imagination: was it one dedicated primarily to "horizontal" relations, to a vision of social peace and harmony beyond tructures of domination and belligerence, or one involved primarily with the "vertical" axis of human–divine encounter? According to this more religious conception of the utopian imagination, the key object of its preoccupations is not so much the overcoming of social hierarchies as a condition in which mortals would once more have at their disposal "holy names," the means with which to address and be addressed by the divine.[7] But even if one were willing to integrate

6. Walter Benjamin, *Illuminations. Essays and Reflections*, trans. Harry Zohn (New York: Schocken, 1989), 262.

7. Hölderlin speaks of the absence of *"heilige Namen"* in his elegy *"Heimkunft"* or "Homecoming."

these two perspectives, to synthesize the horizontal and vertical axes of Hölderlin's preoccupations, one would still, I think, run the risk of missing what is distinctive about his poetic imagination. The risk is, ultimately, to understand Hölderlin's project as one of an anticipatory figuration of human and divine harmony, of a new *totality* or *wholeness* within which each would have his part, his voice within the new, sacred choir of humankind. The risk would be, precisely, to think of Hölderlin as a poet of *relational surrender* rather than as one of *ethical encounter*. The result would also represent, I want to suggest, a serious form of depoliticization.

III

In his discussion of the metaethical self in the *Star*, Rosenzweig explicitly differentiates his understanding of its "demonic" aspect from Goethe's figuration of the *Daimon* "where the word designates just the personality" (71).[8] Hölderlin's famous hymn *"Der Rhein"* does, however, resonate powerfully with Rosenzweig's thoughts about the "birthday" of the metaethical self. In the poem, the emergence of the self, in contrast with the personality, is figured in the shape of heroic destinies—above all that of Rousseau and Hölderlin's friend, Isaac von Sinclair—as well as in the course of the Rhine river. The fourth strophe of the hymn presents the birth of the river's *daimon* as a paradigmatic scene of enigmatic emergence:

> A riddle, the pure of source. Which
> Even song may scarce disclose. For
> As you began, so shall you remain,
> And though need
> And nurture leave their mark,
> It all depends on birth,
> On the ray of light
> The newborn meets. . . . [9]

8.   Rosenzweig is alluding here to Goethe's poem *"Daimon"* from the cycle, *"Urworte. Orphisch"* ("Primal Words. Orphic").

9.   *Hymns and Fragments by Friedrich Hölderlin*, trans. Richard Sieburth (Princeton: Princeton University Press, 1984), 71. Subsequent references to the poem are to Sieburth's translation.

The emergence of the "heroic destiny" figured here is linked not so much to a natural endowment as to the contingent make-up of what we might call the *ethico-erotic space*—the "ray of light"—surrounding the individual in its infancy (we might note that the third line even speaks the tautological "formula" of the metaethical self: $B = B$). Nature is posited here not as a realm of forces in balance, but rather as one that includes a kind of internal excess; the "heroic" break with nature is immanent to nature itself.

The notion of the metaethical self might also be linked to the Heraclitian formula, *Hen Diapheron Heauto* ("*Das Eine in Sich Unterschiedene*," "the one differentiated in itself"), to which Plato refers in the *Symposium* and which Hölderlin, in his novel *Hyperion*, endorses as the very definition of beauty without which even philosophy would not be possible.[10] If we understand this formula "metaethically," we arrive at an emphatically postclassical conception of art and beauty. Here the accomplishment of the beautiful is conceived not as a harmonization of parts within an ordered whole but rather as the representation of an interrupted whole—or better, a *self-interrupting whole*—one animated, as it were, by a "too much" of pressure from within its midst. Beauty is, in this view, not the achievement of balance and symmetry—not, that is, some form of aesthetic totalization. But nor is it a merely melancholic or romantically ironic index of the incomplete aspect of all human endeavors, an aesthetically rendered insistence on the fragmentation constitutive of human existence. Rather it is one of the occasions, one of the ways in which the defenses that keep human beings from inhabiting the midst of life can be disarmed. That is, beautiful objects are *disarming* not in the sense of releasing us, once and for all, from the "too much" of excitation that is, at some level, constitutive of human life, but rather in the sense of loosening our defenses, opening beyond our stuckness in an especially rigid and defensive organization of this pressure.[11] The combination of quickening and release occa-

---

10. See Friedrich Hölderlin, *Hyperion and Selected Poems*, ed. Eric L. Santner (New York: Continuum, 1990), 67.

11. This is not to say that art is not tempted—even constitutively tempted—by such a project. Perhaps the most famous and most exalted example of succumbing to this temptation is Wagner's music dramas. These works attempt both to intensify and to purge, once and for all, this excitation from the "poetico-musical system" that

sioned by a beautiful object can be understood as the vitality that emerges when this organization is loosened.

It is in this spirit that I read Hölderlin's evocation of the *"Brautfest,"* the marriage of men and gods, toward the end of "The Rhine." The momentary release from the constraints of fate expressed in this figure—"And for a while / Fate achieves a balance"— ought not be understood as a vision of the harmonized corporate community, of the concrete "universality" of the social body divided into parts; it marks instead, to use Rosenzweig's language, the opening *into life* which, as the final strophe's reference to Hölderlin's friend, the political revolutionary Isaac von Sinclair, indicates, continues to be a place of struggle and dispute. Indeed, in the final lines of the poem, Sinclair is celebrated for his (divinely blessed) capacity to dwell in the most difficult aspect of struggle, the caesura or "night" between orders or epochs, the chaos and disorientation that mark the *states of emergence* of the new:

> and the Lord's
> Smile never escapes you
> By day, when life
> Appears fevered and chained,
> Or by night, when everything blends
> Into confusion, and primeval
> Chaos reigns once more.

The penultimate strophe of the poem acknowledges the difficulties of sustaining this opening, of not falling back into a rigidly defensive posture, this or that form of "idolatry." The strophe ends with an allusion to the *Symposium* and the figure of Socrates as the embodiment of a life lived without such defenses:

> The eternal gods are full of life
> At all times; but a man
> Can also keep the best in mind
> Even unto death,
> Thus experiencing the Highest.

stands in for life itself. I would suggest that Wagner's protofascist and above all anti-Semitic political tendencies are directly linked to the nature of this project.

Yet to each his measure.
For misfortune is heavy
To bear, and fortune weighs yet more.
But a wise man managed to stay lucid
Throughout the banquet,
From noon to midnight,
Until the break of dawn.

Rosenzweig's view of revelation helps us understand what has been a fundamental misconception of Hölderlin's poetic efforts.[12] They have been, to use terms suggested by Rosenzweig, understood as poetic expressions of the "old thinking," thinking obsessed with the arche and telos of history, thinking that posits history and human experience as forming some sort of delimited domain beyond which a kind of life would still be possible.[13] I want to insist, by contrast, that Hölderlin was very much a poet of the middle of life, a poet whose courage—or diffidence—can be defined as an opening to this middle, to this being-in-the-midst-of-life, that the Rhine hymn associated with Socratic virtue.[14]

In this context, we might note the affinities between the view of aesthetics I am proposing here and Elaine Scarry's recent work on the ethical and political consequences of aesthetic experience.[15] In

---

12.   Again, the paradox is that we only come to see this misconception as one in light of Rosenzweig's work; it was, as it were, not a misconception prior to Rosenzweig. Such is the peculiar historicity of aesthetic objects.

13.   Heidegger's readings of Hölderlin are also dedicated to establishing the poet's work as the basis of a new, nonmetaphysical mode of thinking. In the present context, I will be limiting myself to what I take to be a more Rosenzweigian idiom of this thinking.

14.   I am alluding here, of course, to Hölderlin's odes, "The Poet's Courage" and its later revision, "Diffidence," to which Walter Benjamin dedicated an early and difficult essay. For Benjamin, too, what is at stake is the thought of what it means to expose oneself to the midst of life, which Benjamin correlates with the "submission to the danger that threatens the world." Walter Benjamin, "Two Poems by Friedrich Hölderlin," in *Walter Benjamin. Selected Writings. Volume 1: 1913–1926*, ed. Michael Jennings and Marcus Bullock, trans. Stanley Corngold (Cambridge: Harvard University Press, 1996), 33.

15.   Elaine Scarry, *On Beauty and Being Just* (Princeton: Princeton University Press, 1999). Subsequent references are given in the text.

her compelling and idiosyncratic essay, Scarry takes up the Idealist insistence on the centrality of beauty to the moral education of humankind. Indeed, the essay is in part an effort to cast Schiller's letters on aesthetic education into a new and less rigidly Kantian idiom. For Scarry, beauty in nature and in art has the capacity to lead the perceiver "to a more capacious regard for the world," a regard in which two meanings of the word *fairness* become in some sense synonymous: comely, lovely to behold; just and equitable (48). Beauty, Scarry argues, forms a locus or agency of *interpellation* in which aesthetics, ethics, and even politics become alloyed. It "intensifies the pressure we feel to repair existing injuries" (57) and bears within itself a "distributional mandate," calling upon us to extend the perceptual care we bring to the beautiful object to a "more capacious sphere of objects" (82). As with Rosenzweig, what is at stake here is our relation to *the source of animation* in what is other. Beauty, she writes, "seems to place requirements on us for attending to the aliveness or (in the case of objects) quasi-aliveness of our world, and for entering into its protection" (90).

For all their similarities, however, Scarry's view of "fairness" differs in one fundamental way from the Rosenzweigian/Hölderlinian perspective I am proposing. For Scarry, the ethical and political energies of beauty are linked to the beautiful object's exemplification of the principle of symmetry, its perceptible figuration of balance, its harmonization of parts within a whole. Beauty is able to quicken our commitment to justice, Scarry argues, because "in periods when a human community is too young to have had time to create justice, as well as in periods when justice has been taken away, beautiful things . . . hold steadily visible the manifest good of equality and balance" (97). The symmetry manifest in the beautiful object serves, in other words, as an insistent placeholder for the imperatives of distributive justice in our social arrangements; the beautiful object, in its symmetrical arrangement of parts within a whole, is an indispensable catalyst for a transferable sensitivity to more general concerns of symmetry and just distribution. For Scarry, the beautiful object is disarming because it figures, in a world marked by unequal distribution, the complementarity of forces and energies, the "One-Differentiated-in-Itself" in the sense of the social body harmoniously divided into parts. A work opens a movement toward ethical and political consciousness because it figures an equipoise and symmetry missing from the rest of life.

What is missing from Scarry's perspective is an appreciation for the dimension of the *remnant* immanent to the beautiful, for an aesthetics of what I have referred to as the interrupted or self-interrupting whole. What is beautiful, in the view I am proposing, moves us because its own formal composition and procedures produce more reality than it can contain. Scarry's universe is ultimately one of what Rosenzweig referred to as relational surrender, of *Hingabe*. There is conceptual room here for the (harmonized) *personality* but not the singular, out-of-joint *self* that provides, as Rosenzweig argues, the basis of any genuine ethical encounter. In a sense, Scarry has gone as far as one could within the framework of the "old thinking." One of the sites where this thinking has most dominated our understanding of Hölderlin's work—and the conception of beauty it manifests—has been the interpretation of the final line of his late hymn of and to memory, *"Andenken"* ("Remembrance"). That line pertains to the poet's essential relation to the remnant (which, as I have suggested, is something different from a fragment): *"Was bleibet aber, stiften die Dichter"* ("But poets establish what remains").[16]

IV

For good reason, *"Andenken"* has been read as a return to the world of *Hyperion* to which it contains various allusions, most importantly, the name "Bellarmin"—"But where are my friends? Bellarmin / With his companion?"—the figure to whom the hero of Hölderlin's epistolary novel addresses his letters. Just as in the novel the realm of heroes and seafarers, represented by the figure Alabanda, and that of lovers, represented by Diotima, are seen to be *aufgehoben* in Hyperion's comprehensive consciousness of the totality of life's paths and aspects, so too in *"Andenken"* are the particular joys and sorrows of sailors and lovers—functions of imperfect dwelling or *Bleiben*—seen to be mastered and, as it were, put in their proper place in life's total-

16. *Hymns and Fragments*, trans. Sieburth, 109. Subsequent references to the poem are to Sieburth's translation.

ity on the basis of a progressive cultivation or *Bildung* of internaliz-
ing remembrance. The lines culminating in Hölderlin's most famous
gnomic utterance are:

> . . . But memory
> Is taken and given by the ocean,
> And the eyes of love do not waver in their gaze,
> But poets establish what remains.

In his compelling and highly influential reading of the poem, the
great Hölderlin scholar Jochen Schmidt has summarized the "Hyp-
erionesque" interpretation in the following terms:

> Poetic "remembrance" is a process involving a transformation
> of consciousness the crucial agents of which are 'love' and
> 'deeds'; the consciousness . . . which ultimately emerges, inte-
> grates the stages of its own becoming by sublimating them in
> a higher and more comprehensive context of relations. . . .
> Only from within this sovereign consciousness with its capac-
> ity to master temporality and integrate each concrete particu-
> lar does that which is set forth in the poem, which is, as the
> particular, now mediated with the whole, attain a final validity.
> Insofar as the poet's consciousness has assumed the form of
> the Absolute he creates *sub specie aeternitatis,* he establishes
> what remains.[17]

Schmidt has reiterated and amplified this reading in his magisterial
commentary on the poem in the recent critical edition of Hölderlin's
works he edited for the *Bibliothek Deutsche Klassiker.* There Schmidt
emphasizes Hölderlin's involvement with the conception of poetic
genius that dominated German letters at the end of the eighteenth
century. This notion is linked, in turn, to that of the "intellectual
intuition." Such an "intuitive perception of totality" guides the poet
in the formation of a consciousness that can then mediate concrete
particulars with respect to this totality; on the basis of such a consciousness the poet is "able to establish what remains insofar as he
brings what is otherwise isolated and lost—untethered from any

---

17. Jochen Schmidt, *Hölderlins letzte Hymnen: "Andenken" und "Mnemosyne"*
(Tübingen: Max Niemeyer, 1970), 40.

meaning—into a relation to the Whole which first endows it with meaning." The deeds of sailors (and other heroes) and lovers are seen as deficient with respect to the human longing for endurance, for *was bleibet*; only the poetic word introduces human life into the order of what truly endures by opening onto a form of sovereign self-possession and mastery: "The hymn presents a movement of thought which unfolds itself in the course of remembrance—a *process* of consciousness leading to the highest form of self-consciousness."[18]

In light of Rosenzweig's metaethics of singularity, it becomes possible, however, to read the final line of *"Andenken"* not as an utterance pertaining to the institution of a totalizing gaze or sovereign consciousness, to the "foundation and augmentation" of enduring meanings and values, but rather as a statement about poetry's crucial role in sustaining what I have referred to as the logic of the remnant. What remains is precisely that: the remnant, the part that is not a part of a whole but rather the opening beyond the "police order" of parts and wholes. What poets establish is not some sort of vision or consciousness of the All; rather they introduce into the relational totality of social existence—into the social body divided into parts— the perspective of "non-all."[19] This refers, once again, not to some place or experience of exception, some locus of authentic life outside the part–whole logic of social relations, but rather, to use a Kabbalistic formulation, to the sparks or blessings of "more life" *within* those relations, which can be liberated from their undeadness by the intervention of the right word. Poets, Hölderlin argues, are the ones who provide us with these right words.[20] And as Hölderlin suggests in *"Andenken,"* such words emerge in relation to and on the basis of human finitude.

18. *Friedrich Hölderlin. Sämtliche Werke und Briefe*, ed. Jochen Schmidt (Frankfurt am Main: Deutsche Klassiker Verlag, 1992), 1:1017, 1018.

19. The sociality at issue here is one which, as Levinas has put it, "in opposition to all knowledge and all immanence, is a *relation with the other as such* and not with the other *as a pure part of the world.*" Emmanuel Levinas, *Basic Philosophical Writings*, ed. Adriaan Peperzak, Simon Critchley, and Robert Bernascoin (Bloomington: Indiana University Press, 1996), 158; emphasis added.

20. Against this background, psychoanalytic interventions are not merely interpretations—constative utterances—but also, at least when they succeed, a modality of poetic performance.

The third strophe of *"Andenken"* speaks of the dangers of "mortal thoughts" [*sterbliche Gedanken*] as well as of the possibility of a life with them:

> It is no good
> To let mortal thoughts
> Rob you of your soul. Yet
> Dialogue is good and to speak
> The heart, to hear all
> About the days of love
> And deeds that have taken place.

Jochen Schmidt reads "mortal thoughts" as a deficient mode of mindedness the overcoming of which is the task of poetic and philosophical speech; the true calling of humans, according to the philosophical tradition to which Hölderlin belongs, is to think what is immortal and divine.[21] According to this reading, Hölderlin's lines—and the poem more generally—can be heard to echo Schiller's call, in his poem *"Das Ideal und das Leben"* ("The Ideal and Life"), to throw off the fears of earthly existence:

> *Wollt ihr hoch auf ihren Flügeln schweben,*
> *Werft die Angst des Irdischen von euch!*
> *Fliehet aus dem engen, dumpfen Leben*
> *In des Idealen Reich!*[22]

> If you wish to glide high on the wings [of spiritual form],
> Throw off the fear of things earthly!
> Flee from the dark and narrow life
> Into the Kingdom of the Ideal!

In his compelling study of the matrix of affinities between Rosenzweig and Heidegger, Peter Gordon has noted the complex fate of

---

21. Schmidt cites in this context, among other sources, Aristotle's *Nicomachean Ethics* (1177 b 33): "But we must not follow those who advise us, being men, to think of human things and, being mortal, of mortal things, but must, so far as we can, make ourselves immortal, and strain every nerve to live in accordance with the best thing in us. . . ." *The Basic Works of Aristotle*, ed. Richard McKeon, trans. W. D. Ross (New York: Random House, 1941), 1105.

22. Quoted in Benno von Wiese, *Deutsche Gedichte. Von den Anfängen bis zur Gegenwart* (Düsseldorf: Pädagogischer Verlag Schwann-Bagel, 1982), 261–62.

these Schillerian verses in the genealogy of the "new thinking" with which Rosenzweig identified himself.[23] In the famous 1929 disputation between Heidegger and Ernst Cassirer at Davos, Cassirer cited Schiller's poem in defense of his understanding of the Kantian legacy, which was among the matters of dispute with Heidegger; to throw off the anxiety of earthly existence is, Cassirer noted, "the position of idealism which I have always confessed as my own."[24] According to Rosenzweig, it was precisely this position with which "the new thinking" had broken. The debates at Davos became—and not only for Rosenzweig—one of the sites where the fault lines of this rupture found clear and dramatic articulation. In the course of his own response to the Cassirer–Heidegger confrontation, Rosenzweig cites a letter of his philosophical mentor, Hermann Cohen, the great Neo-Kantian whose ultimate philosophical legacy belongs, Rosenzweig suggests, on the side of the "new thinking":

> For what else is it when Heidegger, against Cassirer, gives to philosophy the task to reveal to man, "the specifically finite being," his own "nothingness in spite of his freedom" and to "recall him back, into the hardness of his fate, from the shallow aspect of a man who merely uses the work of the spirit"— what is this concluding formulation of the philosophical task other than that passionate representation of the "Individuum quand même" against the "Learned-Bourgeois-Thought" that one must "honor the thinker in the soul and accordingly look upon the intellectual transport towards the eternity of culture as the supreme power and the authentic value of the poor human individual" (Cohen's letter to Stadler upon the death of Gottfried Keller) . . . ?[25]

23. Peter Gordon, "Under One Tradewind: Philosophical Expressionism from Rosenzweig to Heidegger" (Ph.D. diss., University of California, Berkeley, 1997).

24. Ibid., 403. A German transcription of the debate can be found in Martin Heidegger, *Kant und das Problem der Metaphysik* (Frankfurt am Main: Vittorio Klostermann, 1973). A rather poor English translation of that transcription may be found in an appendix to Richard Taft's rendering of the Heidegger volume, *Kant and the Problem of Metaphysics* (Bloomington: Indiana University Press, 1990).

25. Franz Rosenzweig, "Vertauschte Fronten," in *Der Mensch und sein Werk. Gesammelte Schriften*, ed. Reinhold Mayer and Annemarie Mayer (Dordrecht: Mar-

As Gordon goes on to note, in this letter to August Stadler, Cohen had himself appealed to a logic of the remnant in its correlation with human finitude. What is of deepest worth in a human being is, as Cohen puts it there, what *"remains behind"* the "intellectual flight into the eternity of culture"; it is precisely this remnant, Cohen suggests, that holds the place of "the eternal in the earthly."[26] All of this represents, of course, a radical critique of the *Bildungsideologie,* the ideology of culture and self-perfection, that so powerfully informed German-Jewish culture in the post-Enlightenment era.

Finally, as Gordon also reminds us, Rosenzweig himself, as it were, anticipated Cassirer's reference to Schiller's poem in the first lines of the *Star.* There, we recall, Rosenzweig insists on the facticity of death in the face of all philosophical and, we might add, aesthetic attempts at its symbolic elaboration/metabolization. The first sentences of the *Star,* the introductory chapter of which is entitled "On the Possibility of the Cognition of the All," read,

> All cognition of the All originates in death, in the fear of death. Philosophy takes it upon itself to throw off the fear of things earthly [*die Angst des Irdischen abzuwerfen*], to rob death of its poisonous sting, and Hades of its pestilential breath. All that is mortal lives in this fear of death; every new birth augments the fear by one new reason, for it augments what is mortal. (3)

Against this background, I suggest that *"sterbliche Gedanken,"* the "mortal thoughts" that are of concern to Hölderlin in his poem *"Andenken,"* are not simply indications of a failure on the part of man to achieve "the intellectual transport towards the eternity of culture" established in and through the poetic (and, in a different register, philosophical) word; they are, rather, ciphers for the death-driven singularity of human being which can either rob us of our soul—

tinus Nijhoff, 1984), 3:235–37; I am using Peter Gordon's translation ("Under One Tradewind," 440). Gordon discusses at some length the newspaper account of the debates on which Rosenzweig depended (Rosenzweig was, of course, completely paralyzed at this point and died shortly thereafter). The author of the account, published in the *Frankfurter Zeitung,* was Hermann Herrigal, who had read and admired Rosenzweig's work and considered himself a member of the circle of "new thinkers."

26. Quoted in Gordon, "Under One Tradewind," 443.

undeaden our being—or be taken up in the encounter with the neighbor, thereby becoming the very occasion of our ensoulment: "Yet / Dialogue is good and to speak / The heart . . . " [Doch gut / Ist ein Gespräch und zu sagen / Des Herzens Meinung . . .]. If *"Andenken"* speaks, as Schmidt suggests, *sub specie aeternitatis,* then it does so in the sense invoked by Cohen and endorsed by Rosenzweig: under the aspect of, from the perspective of, the "eternal in the earthly." And it is precisely such a perspective and the mode of subjectification proper to it that can, both individually and collectively, open the possibility for new possibilities of being-together, which is, in the end, the very heart of politics.